Direct Mail
In A Week

Patrick Forsyth runs Touchstone Training & Consultancy, an independent firm specializing in the improvement of marketing, sales and communications skills, based in the UK.

He has visited and worked regularly in South East Asia for more than 20 years, and has conducted programmes for the Singapore Institute of Management and other training providers in Singapore, Indonesia, Hong Kong and Thailand.

He has presented public programmes for organizations such as the Institute of Management, City University Business School, London Chamber of Commerce, and the London Management Centre.

In addition, his in-company training experience spans many different industries and he also writes extensively on management matters. He is the author of many successful business books (such as *100 Great Sales Ideas* and *How to Write Reports and Proposals*) and writes regularly for a number of business journals including *Better Business* and *Professional Marketing*.

Teach® Yourself

Direct Marketing In A Week

Patrick Forsyth

First published in Great Britain in 2014 by Hodder & Stoughton. An Hachette UK company.

This edition published in US in 2016 by Quercus

This edition published in Great Britain in 2016 by John Murray Learning

Copyright © Patrick Forsyth 2014, 2016

The right of Patrick Forsyth to be identified as the Author of the Work has been asserted by him in accordance with the Copyright, Designs and Patents Act 1988.

Database right Hodder & Stoughton (makers)

The *Teach Yourself* name is a registered trademark of Hachette UK.

British Library Cataloguing in Publication Data: a catalogue record for this title is available from the British Library.

Library of Congress Catalog Card Number: on file.

Paperback ISBN: 978 1473 60954 9

eBook ISBN: 978 1444 79513 4

1

The publisher has used its best endeavours to ensure that any website addresses referred to in this book are correct and active at the time of going to press. However, the publisher and the author have no responsibility for the websites and can make no guarantee that a site will remain live or that the content will remain relevant, decent or appropriate.

The publisher has made every effort to mark as such all words which it believes to be trademarks. The publisher should also like to make it clear that the presence of a word in the book, whether marked or unmarked, in no way affects its legal status as a trademark.

Every reasonable effort has been made by the publisher to trace the copyright holders of material in this book. Any errors or omissions should be notified in writing to the publisher, who will endeavour to rectify the situation for any reprints and future editions.

Typeset by Cenveo® Publisher Services.

Printed and bound in Great Britain by CPI Group (UK) Ltd, Croydon, CR0 4YY.

John Murray Learning policy is to use papers that are natural, renewable and recyclable products and made from wood grown in sustainable forests. The logging and manufacturing processes are expected to conform to the environmental regulations of the country of origin.

John Murray Learning
Carmelite House
50 Victoria Embankment
London
EC4Y 0DZ
www.hodder.co.uk

Contents

Introduction

Picking the right promotional mix is not easy. Whatever is done it must be effective, and also cost-effective, and both budgets and time are no doubt limited. Business does not arrive unbidden (or very little of it does), nor does it magically arrive just by crossing your fingers and shouting 'Promotion!'; so something must be done and time and effort must be expended to make sure it works.

Even in this electronic age, direct mail remains a popular form of promotion. It can certainly find and hold customers and do so cost-effectively too. But, you may have noticed, it does not have the best image – the words 'junk mail' are frequently used in relation to direct mail offerings!

However, used carefully, it can work for seller and buyer alike. This book sets out how to utilize direct marketing for maximum benefit for both.

Direct mail is simply a marketing, promotional technique like any other, but it certainly has the ability to ignite strong feelings, not all of them positive. Everyone appears to know someone who has been mailed about something inappropriate, or addressed wrongly as 'Dear Madam' (or 'Dear Sir', depending on the correct gender). Everything here is thus pitched not just to make its use effective, but to make its use acceptable. One is no good without the other.

Success in many things is in the detail and that is certainly true of direct mail. Indeed, I once saw research that said that, faced with a mailshot, a reader takes just two and a half seconds to decide whether to look at it further or ditch it. That's quite a challenge for the writer of such a piece. It was Samuel Johnson who said, 'What is written without effort is in general read without pleasure', and certainly the words used to convey the message of any direct mail must be clear, persuasive and more (as we shall see). So some of this book focuses on actually writing the message. Surely writing is easy, especially when you are describing something you know well, like your product or service. Right, but look at the evidence. For example, information about a cross-channel ferry service announces: 'Shuttles leave every half hour ... on the hour'! This was presumably originated not only by a poor writer, but someone with a pretty odd clock! Perhaps my favourite example of such mistakes is a sign in a Nottinghamshire hotel, which reads, 'In the interests of security bedroom doors must be locked before entering or leaving the room'. A good trick if you can do it ... or evidence of a fifth dimension, perhaps? This sign had been written, printed and placed on the inside of 256 bedrooms, all apparently without anyone noticing that it was nonsense.

Remember, both the examples just mentioned (and one could mention so many more) are only a single sentence. If it is difficult to get that much right, then perhaps writers can be forgiven for struggling to complete a full description of their product, why someone should buy it and how they can do so.

The so-called 'MEGO effect' (Makes Eyes Glaze Over) is all too easy to invoke. For direct mail to work, and work well, you have to get the words that express your ideas down in a correct, clear, original and pleasing way, and the only way to do that is to check, check and check again. Read it over on screen, read it over having printed it out, read it out loud to yourself, read it out loud to someone else; do all this twice. And when you have done any editing this necessitates, do it all again. A systematic approach to all this is described in these pages.

In addition, a host of other factors must be right too. Each element is, of itself, not complex; there are core principles here that make it straightforward and manageable to create good direct mail ... and to reap the benefits. The trick of any good promotion is to create and maintain interest in potential buyers and prompt action. That action can take many forms: requesting more information, talking to someone – in person or by telephone – or visiting a website and more. Some promotional methods can prompt direct sales and direct mail is one of them. In some kinds of business it is possible to send a mailshot and measure its success in orders, and perhaps payments, arriving back in response.

In addition, what is done must relate appropriately to overall marketing strategy and to other elements of the business and of the promotional mix. For example, as I started to write this my morning post brought a brochure. It prompted me to check the organization's website, then telephone (with a query the website did not answer) and place an order, paying by credit card. Although more than just the brochure was involved, this would be judged a success from the point of view of the sender – and from mine too, I hope!

One vital link these days is via electronic communication, and so included here is a chapter about the close overlap that now exists with email marketing (see Friday's chapter).

If you position the use of direct mail effectively within the totality of your promotional mix, and make it work well – and that means systematically making sure that every element of it works well, from a letter and brochure to an envelope and much more – it can be an important part of your business-generating process. In this book, in seven succinct chapters, we review how to make that so.

Patrick Forsyth

www.patrickforsyth.com

SUNDAY

The recipients: database considerations

Whether simple or more complex, direct mail must always be approached in the right way. What makes it successful? The answer, in a few words, is attention to detail. And it is not just the words but everything that matters: whom you mail, what you send, how the message is put over and the way in which customers are asked to respond.

Any promotion needs to be well directed, and there is an old saying that you are after the MAN – whoever has the Money, the Authority to commit and the Need. Direct mail is essentially promotion by post, and its close relations include putting brochures as inserts in magazines and delivering door to door. Its particular nature means it is potentially:

- personal (essentially it can put a message in front of individuals)
- flexible (it can involve mailing any number of 'shots': 40, 400, 4,000, 40,000 or more)
- specific (it can deliver messages tailored to different groups and individuals)
- controllable (and easy to assess how well it is working).

It is also a form of promotion that can be low cost, small scale and ideally suited to low-budget marketing and smaller businesses. It will, in fact, do many things, prompting business from prospects, maintaining business from existing customers and much in between.

First things first: direct mail is only a particular form of advertising – promotion by post. The term encompasses all the elements of the promotional message delivered in this way – brochures, letters, envelopes and how to orchestrate a persuasive message and create a direct mail 'shot' or an entire campaign.

Despite its 'junk mail' moniker, direct mail is used successfully by a wide range of companies, most of them perfectly respectable. Such companies include charities, accountants and publishers, as well as producers of a wide range of products and services, in organizations large and small.

Used effectively, it can produce good results and, carried out carefully and systematically, it can certainly be cost-effective. Some very simple, low-cost, approaches are possible. For example, as I was thinking about writing this, a postcard arrived from a hotel I have stayed in (and like). This is a good 'reminder' promotion, one addressed to people known to the company and who know the product. I have received similar communications, aimed at keeping a particular management conference centre in the mind of the recipient. (One such card had six pictures linked to summer events; others have used dramatic pictures such as a striking close-up of a rare breed of pig raised in the grounds.) Another promotional postcard I received recently consisted solely of an invitation to visit a website (and made it sound like a useful thing to do).

What makes direct mail successful?

We will review these matters in turn. First, you have to have someone, or many 'someones', to whom to send your direct mail.

Prospects – selecting respondents

It will always bring better results if your mailshots are addressed to individual prospects, and that means by name, not 'The Managing Director, ABC Co. Ltd'.

The effectiveness of any mailing is clearly dependent on mailing the right people, i.e. on the quality of the mailing list.

There are two approaches to the question of lists: either build your own or use other people's (or a combination of both, as they are not mutually exclusive).

Outside sources of lists abound, available most often for rent, and sometimes for outright purchase. Rented lists are well guarded and will always include what are called 'seeded' names, that is, names placed in the list to allow the owner to monitor how it is used. Such lists might include the home addresses of certain members of the renter's staff. This prevents lists hired for one-time use being copied and used again. Using outside lists can be very useful, not least because it avoids the problem of holding them, printing off labels and much of the administrative detail involved. Sources of lists are well documented and these days just putting 'direct mail lists' in Google will produce links to many sources for rent or purchase.

At the same time, informal sources, ranging from companies you know to chambers of trade or commerce, may also be useful. In addition, you can cull names from a wealth of directories (those that do not make their entries available in list form), not simply to mail once, but to record and use again. For many the most valuable sector of their list is not prospects but actual customers.

Holding and maintaining lists

Mailing lists are a perishable commodity. They have to be maintained and updated. The latter is important: people move jobs, position and location and like to be addressed correctly. While all customers and enquirers (everyone from a telephone enquirer to someone met at a conference or exhibition) need to go on your list, you may need to clean names out after a period of no response. But be careful: I know one company that has a kind of 'last chance' category, those they continue to mail for just a little longer, and another that refers to LYBUNTs (standing for Last Year, But Unfortunately Not This in terms of orders). The biggest order I have ever received came after a past customer was kept on the list for just over three years without response, so choose cut-off points carefully.

Once, small-scale direct mail involved manual systems, card indexes and the like. Now for all practical purposes – and for any real quantity – list holding necessitates a computer. As a result most (even quite small) systems are able to hold lists and can be programmed with additional facilities (for instance, mail-merging systems which allow letters to be produced with the name on the label used in the letter).

Computer companies and their distributors will be only too willing to offer help and advice. If you have an existing system, the new element must be compatible with it and, while there is a profusion of good standard software available, it is important that this will give you the exact operation you want.

For example, you may wish to:

- print out by company/organization as well as individual names
- rebate-sort, i.e. to deliver post to the post office pre-sorted in a way that qualifies for lower rates (though note that it also takes longer to deliver)
- link into other record systems, clients, debtors, etc.
- print quietly or at a certain speed.

Or you may simply want to avoid your labels looking as if they have come off a computer system.

MONDAY TUESDAY WEDNESDAY THURSDAY FRIDAY SATURDAY

Do not be seduced by all the many things computers can do (or by technical enthusiasts). You want a system to do all the things you want, but you do not want it full of irrelevancies, and over complicated to operate and keep up to date.

All the caveats of purchasing this sort of equipment apply. Like all such systems, exactly what will suit you needs some investigation. Even when you do, then as the saying has it, 'When your system works well, it's obsolete'. I will make no attempt here to itemize specific equipment or software, as what is available changes while you watch. But this is no excuse not to make decisions to buy. However long you wait, there will always be a better system available tomorrow.

Think ahead: you will never anticipate everything as technology moves so fast, but do not be caught out by adopting too narrow a focus and failing to incorporate some actually easily predictable element of what your system must do.

Data protection and the law

While this is not the place to go into lengthy technical detail (and things change), there are considerations to be borne in mind regarding the legal aspects of data protection. The Direct Marketing Association (UK) Limited (DMA) describes itself as Europe's largest trade association in the marketing and communications sector, with approximately 900 corporate members and positioned in the top 5 per cent of UK trade associations by income. It represents both advertisers, who market their products using direct marketing techniques, and specialist suppliers of direct marketing services to those advertisers – for example, advertising agencies, outsourced contact centres, etc. The DMA also administers the Mailing

Preference Service, the Telephone Preference Service and the Fax Preference Service. On behalf of its membership, the DMA promotes best practice, through its Direct Marketing Code of Practice, in order to maintain and enhance consumers' trust and confidence in the direct marketing industry. The Direct Marketing Association is an independent body that monitors industry compliance. It may be worth readers visiting their website, www.dma.org.uk, for further information.

The industry they represent is huge: the total value of direct marketing to the UK economy was estimated to be £9.1 billion in 2011. This comprises three separate figures: £4.3 billion on expenditure on direct marketing media and activities, £1.1 billion on goods and services bought in by companies to enable the undertaking of direct marketing activity and £3.7 billion through the spending of people employed in the industry as consumers ('Putting a Price on Direct Marketing', *The DMA*, July 2012).

I asked them what key factors direct mailers need to be aware of regarding the Data Protection Act 1998; they listed the following (NB: reference to sections and principles can lead you to the full text of the Act, though a summary should suffice):

● The need to ensure that any personal data used (e.g. name and address details) are:
  a) accurate and up to date (principle 4) (old/inaccurate data is a key problem in this sector)
  b) only being used for the purpose for which they were captured (principle 2) (failure to properly permission data, e.g. to provide a clear opt-out for direct marketing by mail, is a common problem, especially when the data is to be used by third parties for marketing purposes)
  c) not used for marketing if the data subject has requested that it not be used in this fashion (see section 11) (see also the MPS – Mailing Preference Service. Use of this is not strictly a legal requirement but it is now effectively a requirement as it demonstrates a data subject's request not to have their personal data processed for the purpose of direct marketing by mail)

d) kept secure, so protected against unauthorized or unlawful access, use, loss, destruction or damage

e) not being processed (e.g. held on a server) outside the EEA unless adequate protections are in place (principle 8)

- In addition, data subjects' rights must be respected, such as the right to make a subject access request (see section 7) (see ICO website for Code of practice on these: http://www.ico.org.uk/for_organisations/data_protection/~/media/documents/library/Data_Protection/Detailed_specialist_guides/subject-access-code-of-practice.PDF)

- If sensitive personal data is being used, e.g. data relating to the data subject's health and wellbeing or trade union membership, this must be subject to a higher level of protection to reflect its sensitive nature.

- Direct marketers using direct mail as a channel may be the recipients of a monetary penalty notice levied by the ICO (Information Commissioner's Office) should they commit a breach of the Data Protection Act 1998. The maximum fine is £500,000 – but actual amounts depend on a variety of factors, including the potential risk to the data subjects, the severity of the risk, the number of potentially affected data subjects, and the amount that the organization responsible can afford to pay without being put out of business. The fine will be levied on the data controller rather than the data processor. If the direct mailer is the data processor rather than the data controller this does not mean that they are not at risk, however, if they are responsible for a breach of the Data Protection Act 1998. Normally there will be an agreement in place with the data controller that makes the data processor liable for any such fines that are levied as a result of in/action on the part of the data processor.

As you can see, even from such a potted statement, this is an area that contains pitfalls and may be worthy of care, further study or advice. Be aware, though, that an awful lot of direct mail happens without any problems with the law.

Summary

Several things should be clear early on. First (and this whole book reflects this fact), the success of direct mail is in the detail. Thus it needs some care, and respect for the proven principles, to get it right. Attention needs to be given to all aspects of it, from creating a well-composed persuasive letter to having the right kind of short message on an envelope.

Secondly, direct mail is only as good as the list that directs it. A list is an asset to be nurtured, updated and refined. Address those on it you know best accurately and maintain correct details, for they are likely to be the best respondents.

Finally, although it is not something to panic about, there are controls and the laws of data protection need to be known and respected. Get it right, however, and direct mail is a technique that can work well and profitably.

SUNDAY

MONDAY

TUESDAY

WEDNESDAY

THURSDAY

FRIDAY

SATURDAY

Fact check (answers at the back)

1. At what stage of the pitching process may the client decline?
a) Not until the end ❏
b) Half-way through ❏
c) At *any* stage ❏
d) At first contact ❏

2. What does MEGO stand for?
a) Makes everything disappear ❏
b) Makes eyes glaze over ❏
c) Marketing effectiveness guaranteed online ❏
d) Must effectively get on ❏

3. How often should mailing lists be updated?
a) Regularly ❏
b) Annually ❏
c) Every so often ❏
d) Daily ❏

4. How do you address people to get the best results?
a) By job title ❏
b) By name ❏
c) By job function ❏
d) By organization name ❏

5. How does direct mail work best?
a) Used alone ❏
b) Following advertising ❏
c) (Well) coordinated with all other promotion ❏
d) Linked only to merchandising ❏

6. Which of the following can reduce postal costs?
a) Colour coding ❏
b) Rebate sorting ❏
c) Reversing A–Z order ❏
d) Omitting the stamps ❏

7. Recipients must be well chosen. MAN indicates what?
a) The Money, Authority and Need ❏
b) Mostly Alternative Needs ❏
c) Many Amongst Numbers ❏
d) Maximizing All Needs ❏

8. How should you view Data Protection legislation?
a) Ignore it ❏
b) Forget it ❏
c) Always bear it in mind ❏
d) Check it occasionally ❏

MONDAY

The core elements of direct mail

Two factors are clear solid foundations to success. First, you must be clear about who your promotion addresses and what, precisely, the objectives are of doing so. Clarity at this stage serves to direct all the other preparation necessary and keep it aimed in the right direction. Because direct mail is so affected by the detail of the exact form it takes, a lack of clarity here can misalign what is done and dilute the responses it prompts.

SUNDAY
MONDAY
TUESDAY
WEDNESDAY
THURSDAY
FRIDAY
SATURDAY

A clear intention

The first step, before any mailshot or campaign can be put together, is for you to decide the objectives: what are you looking to prompt? You may say that the answer to this is obvious: you want to sell the firm and its product/services and you want people to buy them. But this may prove too simplistic a view to enable the construction of an effective mailshot.

Promotion may be designed to sell the product, but it is just as likely to be designed to produce:

- enquiries (in whatever form: a telephone call, logging onto your website)
- requests for information
- something that will receive a personal sales follow-up.

Combinations of these intentions and more are possible.

To prompt specific action you must be clear exactly what the product/service is. It is difficult to move from a general description 'We provide market research services' to truly descriptive copy, much less persuasive copy. You must be able to see your company from the customers' point of view.

Knowing how and why customers view you as they do is a prerequisite to putting any promotional material together, especially material for direct mail, which may be distributed widely and contain elements that are retained by recipients or used regularly for some time, as with an accompanying brochure. Taking a view of what a prospect may know or see elsewhere about you, your message may well aim to build on and extend that knowledge.

Having clear objectives for promotion includes having a clear idea of what response you look for as a result of receipt of the 'shot'. Put simply, what do you want recipients *to do* if they are interested?

Of course, one possible action for smaller-scale mailings is telephone follow-up. It is often very effective to say in your letter, 'I will telephone you in a few days' and then take the initiative (perhaps especially when a meeting is the next stage). Otherwise, the need is to offer other options of response which

SUNDAY

MONDAY

TUESDAY

WEDNESDAY

THURSDAY

FRIDAY

SATURDAY

will appeal – and appeal sufficiently to prompt the recipient to take the initiative.

The temptation is perhaps to go for simplicity ('You ring us'), or for what you want most ('Come and see us for a discussion'). The more persuasive you feel your message is, the stronger this temptation may be.

Yet the core principle of empathy must be applied. The response, or responses – many direct mailshots provide a choice – must be made attractive in customer terms. Will they want to send for more information? If so, how much information should we give them now (without solving the problem) and in what form? Will they want to meet you? If so, whom? Where (your offices, theirs or a neutral venue)? Alone? With others (their colleagues, or others who are interested? Would they expect or like to attend an event? Even minor details are important. For example, they may be more likely to phone you if you offer a freephone number or to return a card on which the postage is pre-paid.

Next, even if you plan only small-scale direct mail (and for the small business this may be worth targeting – 'I will send ten letters every week, day or month'), you must create an appropriate message.

Writing the copy

As we saw in the introduction, writing is not easy, especially writing something that must be persuasive. A couple more examples make the point. For a while there was a sign on Paddington station that said: 'Passengers must not leave their luggage unattended at any time or they will be taken away and destroyed.' Once when I checked in at Sydney airport I was handed a printed card which stated: 'Has anyone put anything in your luggage without your knowledge?' (I could only say I didn't know!).

Let's be clear: even one sentence can cause problems – you have been warned! Writing your message needs care and needs checking.

TIP

Check everything you write carefully more than once. Sleep on it, come back to it, get someone else to read it: get it right.

So how do you go about it?

Provide a sound basis of understanding

First things first. No one will buy anything they do not understand, and if something is unclear in a mailshot it will most likely be discarded; checking up to clarify is just seen as too complicated. So clarity is vital. Saying something is *quite nice* is so bland that, if applied to something that is *hugely enjoyable* it understates it by so much as to be almost insulting. The emphasis is inadequate, even though I suppose at least the word *nice* makes it clear that something positive is being said.

Diluting description with blandness is certainly to be avoided; it is unlikely to add power to your case, and choosing the wrong word is another matter. Doing so might confuse, upset – or worse. The following examples are designed to show the danger. Let us start with a couple of simple everyday words: *comic* and *comical*. Mean much the same thing? No.

Something *comic* is intended to be funny, whereas something *comical* is funny unintentionally.

More relevant to business presentations are the following:

- *Continuous* (unbroken or uninterrupted) and *continual* (repeated or recurring) – a project might be continuous (in process all the time), but work on it is more likely to be continual (unless you never sleep).
- Are you *uninterested* in a proposal or *disinterested* in it? The first implies you are apathetic and care not either way, the latter means you have nothing to gain from it.
- Similarly, *dissatisfied* and *unsatisfied* should not be confused; the former means disappointed, while the latter means needing more of something.
- You might want to do something *expeditious* (quick and efficient), but saying it is *expedient* might not be so well regarded as it means only that something is convenient (not always a good reason to do anything).
- *Fortuitous* implies something happening accidentally; it does not mean fortunate.
- If you are a *practical* person then you are effective, if something is *practicable* it is merely possible to do, and *pragmatic* is something meant to be effective (rather than proven to be).

One wrong word may do damage and ill-chosen words can quickly create nonsense: 'This practicable approach will ensure the practicable project will be continuous'; 'It is fortuitous that I am uninterested in it and I am sure I will not be unsatisfied to see it start'.

Of course, no inaccurate or ungrammatical use of language will help your case even if it only annoys rather than confuses (as, for example, saying *very unique* might do – *unique* means unlike anything else and cannot be qualified in this way). Some care, maybe even some checking or study, may be useful.

TIP *Ensure understanding. Think carefully about the words you use and keep a dictionary and a thesaurus close at hand.*

Language that persuades

The whole area of sales psychology is beyond our remit here (you might usefully read another book in this series: *Selling In A Week*). However, certain principles can be mentioned here: one thing that must pervade every aspect of persuasive writing is appropriate language, so do read this. Hang on – simply saying what you want someone to do is not enough. When I wrote above 'read this', then you might well have rejected the instruction out of hand – *shan't*. But if I say that reading it might just help you get your next mailshot to bring in a good response, then you are more likely to begin to take interest because that helps you. This illustrates the first principle. To be persuasive you must offer people *reasons* to agree or act that reflect *their* point of view, not just say why *you* think they should do something. Such an approach demands empathy and must allow people to identify with it and with you. So, some do's and don'ts:

- **Make your case understandable.** First things first, no one will agree to anything they do not understand. And every time someone thinks: 'I'm not quite sure what you mean', they are not just confused by one point, they are adopting a view of someone who is unsure of themselves. Furthermore, making complex issues seem easy always impresses: a good, succinct description can get people saying, 'Seems straightforward so far', and wanting to read more. Like any communication, a persuasive message needs organizing; you need to go through things in a logical order in a way that, while factual and clear, also projects something of yourself. If you want to sound friendly, efficient or professional – whatever – make sure such characteristics show. People agree most readily with those who seem to show that they are to be believed, who have the necessary knowledge, expertise or whatever.

- **Be truly descriptive.** I regularly see examples of business writing that are almost wholly without adjectives. Yet surely one of the first purposes of language is to be *descriptive*. Most writing needs to paint a picture, to some degree at least. Contrast two phrases: *smooth as silk* and *sort of shiny*.

The first (used, now I think of it, as a slogan by Thai Airways) conjures up a clear and precise picture, or certainly does for anyone who has seen and touched silk. The second might mean almost anything; dead wet fish are sort of shiny, but they are hardly to be compared with the touch of silk. Further, an even more descriptive phrase may be required. I once heard someone on the radio describe something as *slippery as a freshly buttered ice-rink*. Could anyone think this meant anything other than *really, really* slippery? Description, good description, can make things (even complicated things) effortlessly clear; and when it does, it is appreciated. And if it is both descriptive and makes something easier to understand than readers expect, they are doubly appreciative. Clear description may need working at, but the effort is worthwhile. Furthermore, while outright description is important, sometimes we want more than that. We want an element of something being descriptive and also *memorable*. It seems to me that this is achieved in two ways: first by something that is descriptive yet unusual, secondly, when it is descriptive and unexpected. For instance, I once saw a mailshot from a charity raising funds for partially sighted people. One of the enclosures was a cloudy sheet of Perspex, with the instruction to 'look through this and you will see exactly how these people must view the world'. Definitely memorable and unequivocal description too.

- **Avoid an introspective tone.** If every thought begins with the word 'I' ('I will ...', 'I can ...', 'I offer ...' and worst of all 'I want ...'(ditto 'we')), it creates a 'catalogue' feeling, listing things from your point of view; it becomes tedious and is unlikely to prompt interest. This is a common fault – look at any material you receive to find examples of this. Try rephrasing any such sentiment starting with the word 'You ...'. It will sound very different. Thus: 'I would like to give you ...' becomes something that begins 'You will find ...'. If the latter continues by explaining *why* people will find something interesting or valuable, better still.
- **Avoid circumspection.** A persuasive tone has no place for '*I think ...*', '*I hope ...*', '*probably*', '*maybe*' or '*perhaps*'. Have the

courage of your convictions. Anything for which you seek agreement must reflect your confidence in it. So phrases like 'this *will* give you ...' are better. Similarly, avoid bland description. Your case is never just 'very good'. Nothing about your proposition should be stated as being 'quite interesting'. Use words and descriptions that add drama and certitude. Attention here can transform a case. The job is to bring your ideas to life, to have people really wanting to hear more about them and recognizing – easily and up front – that they are (if they are) special.

● **Stress the benefits.** *Features* are factual things – tangible or intangible – about something. This small section is c.900 words long, occupies a couple of pages and deals with persuasive language: all these facts are features. *Benefits* are things that something does for or means to people. So the benefits of reading this are: receiving an introduction to a useful aspect of persuasive communication; help in avoiding your making key mistakes that will dilute your persuasive effectiveness; and increasing the chances of your next mailshot prompting many responses. Benefits should always predominate in any message. They should be sufficient to persuade, they should be well expressed and lead the message rather than being tagged on as some sort of afterthought.

SUNDAY

MONDAY

TUESDAY

WEDNESDAY

THURSDAY

FRIDAY

SATURDAY

It is usually best to state benefits first – making your case benefit-led. Features logically fit second, as with 'This frying pan can cook five or six eggs at the same time (benefit), because it's 75 square centimetres (feature)'. In other words, features explain how it is benefits exist. And you can imagine how this sort of description will ring bells with a large family or a café owner.

Additionally, it is often necessary for a case to be backed up by proof or evidence. That is something other than *you* saying so. It includes everything from the opinions of others likely to be respected by whomever you aim to persuade to factual evidence. For example, which is more believable: a car brochure saying 'This model does 45 mpg', or 'Tests by the Automobile Association show that this model does 45 mpg'? Bear in mind that this is only something that carries weight if the potential customer is interested in economical motoring.

So, ensuring that you are persuasive needs some preparation. Think about what you want to say. Ask yourself why anyone should agree to your idea or proposal. List the reasons – all of them. Then organize them. What is most important? Arrange a logical argument: say something at the beginning to command attention and then ensure you maintain interest throughout. A powerful start quickly tailing away will persuade no one. Lead with the benefits. And let features follow to explain. This section will *allow readers to experiment with a more persuasive style* (benefit), because it is *written reflecting proven, practical approaches to communication* (feature). Then, when you do close – *ask* for agreement – increasing your chances of getting it.

Maybe next time you set out to persuade, perhaps you might consider doing some checking .... Oops! Sorry. Next time you want to obtain agreement and commitment, make checking that your case is not just well described, but *persuasively* described, a priority.

That said, you have to get the words down.

A systematic approach to creating copy

The following provides a proven pathway. You can follow it or adapt it. You can shortcut it somewhat, especially for straightforward bits of work, but not too much – omitting significant elements of the different stages can make writing slower, more awkward and allow the end result to be less good than would otherwise be the case.

Stage 1: research

This may or may not be necessary. It may be that everything you need to have to hand is in your head. On the other hand it may be that you need to do some digging, or at the very least some assembling. For example, let us suppose you are writing about one of your company's products. It may make sense to get together previous documents describing it (technical literature, even the product itself), and have these to hand as you commence the job. It may be that you need to cast the net wider; in this case what about examining competitive product material, for example?

There is no hard and fast rule here. You should, however, ask yourself what might be useful and take a moment to collect and look at or read what the task suggests is necessary.

Stage 2: list the content

Next, forgetting about sequence, structure and arrangement, just list – in short note (or keyword) form – every significant point you might want to make. Give yourself plenty of space; certainly use one sheet of paper as it lets you see everything at a glance without turning over. Put the points down, as they occur to you, at random across the page. *Note:* some – many – of these will need to be stated in benefit form (as just discussed).

You will find that this process (which is a form of mindmapping) acts as a good thought prompter. It enables you to fill out the picture as one thing leads to another, with the freestyle approach removing the need to think or worry about anything else or even linking points together. The scale of this stage may vary. Sometimes it is six words on the back of an envelope, more often somewhat more on an A4 sheet.

This book started life on a sheet of flipchart paper divided into squares for the various chapters, so use a larger sheet if necessary.

Stage 3: sorting it out

Now you can bring some sort of order to bear. Review what you have noted down and decide:

- on the sequence in which points should go
- what logically goes together
- what is ancillary, providing illustration, evidence or example to exemplify points made
- whether the list is complete (you may think of things to add), or whether some things on it can be omitted *without* weakening the persuasive case. This latter point links to careful consideration of length (there is more about this later).

The quickest and easiest way to do this is to annotate your original notes, highlighting and amending them in a second colour. This is for your reference only; if you find it helpful to use arrows, circle words or draw symbols or pictures – fine, do so.

Stage 4: arrange the content

Sometimes, at the end of the previous stage, you have a note you can follow and no more is necessary. Often, however, what you have in front of you is a bit of a mess. By 'arranging the content' I mean simply turning it into a neat list; this could also be the stage at which you type it out to finish the job on screen. Most people seem to input their own written material nowadays (I sometimes think the typing is harder work than the writing!).

Final revision is, of course, still possible at this stage but, that done (and it might include getting another opinion about it from a colleague), you are left with a clear list setting out content, sequence, and emphasis to whatever level of detail you find helpful. Some experimentation may be useful here; certainly I am not suggesting over-engineering the process. This sheet is the blueprint from which you write. You must decide the form in which such is most useful.

Stage 5: a final review

This may not always be necessary – or possible (deadlines may be looming) – but it can be useful to leave it a while (sleep on it), and only start writing after you come back to it fresh. You can get very close to things, and it helps you to see it clearly to step back from it and distract your mind with something else.

Now, with a final version of what is effectively your writing plan in front of you, you can – at last – actually draft the text.

Stage 6: writing

Now you write, or type or dictate. This is where the real work is, though it is very much easier with a clear plan for the task. What you have done here is obvious, but significant. You have separated the two tasks, one of deciding *what* to write, the other deciding *how* to put it. Being a bear of very little brain, I for one certainly find this easier; so too do many other people. Some further tips:

● **Choose the right moment.** If possible, pick a time when you are 'in the mood'. There seem to be times when words flow more easily than others. Also, interruptions can disrupt the flow and make writing take much longer as you recap in your mind, get back into something and continue. It is not always possible, of course, but a bit of organization to get as close as possible to the ideal is very worthwhile.
● **Keep writing.** Do not stop and agonize over small details. If you cannot think of the right word, a suitable heading – whatever – put in a row of xxxxxxs and continue; you can always return and fill in the gaps later, but if you lose the whole thread then writing becomes more difficult and takes longer to do. Again the idea of preserving the flow in this way can quickly become a habit, especially if you are convinced it helps.

So now you have a draft, though already you may feel that it needs further work. Now what?

Stage 7: editing

Few – if any – people write perfect text first time and alter nothing. If you write, then some editing goes with the territory. So, rule one is not to feel inadequate, but to accept that this is the way it works and allow a little time for revision. Careful preparation, as suggested in earlier stages, should minimize alterations; at least you should not be finding things you have left out, or needing to alter the whole structure. The words may need work, however. Computer spelling and grammar checkers are very useful but be warned: not every wrong spelling is corrected automatically (for example, *their* and *there*); proper names and suchlike may need care too. Grammar checkers should not be followed slavishly, especially for the punchy style you need for some persuasive messages. Perhaps a sensible rule here is not to ignore anything highlighted as grammatically incorrect *unless* you can give yourself a good reason for doing so.

Editing may be helped by:

● Sleeping on it (as mentioned earlier)
● Getting a colleague to check it (maybe you can do a swap with someone else who would value your looking at some of their written material – it is amazing how a fresh eye and brain picks up things to which you are, or have become, blind. Incidentally, listen to what they say and consider it carefully; it is easy to become automatically defensive and reject what, with hindsight, may turn out to be good advice).
● Being thorough (do not regard editing as a chore; it is an inherent part of getting something right).

Editing is an important stage. Seemingly small changes: replacing a word, breaking a long sentence into two, adding more and better-placed punctuation; all may make a real difference. This is the time to bear in mind style and use of language (see next chapter) as well as sense and clarity. Then, when you are happy with it, let it go – just press 'print' or do whatever comes next. It is easy to tinker forever. You will always think of something else that could be put differently (better?) if you leave it and look again; productivity is important too.

Let your version of this systematic approach become a habit and you will find your writing improves, and that actually writing gets easier and quicker to do. As a rule of thumb, allow a proportion of the total time you allocate, or simply need, for writing for preparation. If you find that, say, 15–30 per cent of the time, whatever works for you, is necessary, you will also find that rather than 'additional' preparation increasing the overall task time, such jobs actually begin to take less time. Simply pitching in and starting immediately at the top of a blank sheet of paper (or computer screen) with no preparation is just *not* the quicker option that perhaps it sometimes seems to be.

If you are conscious of how you write and think about what makes the writing process easier or more difficult for you, then you will no doubt add to this list and adopt further ways that help you. Of course, at the same time we must be realistic. There are things that interfere with how you would like to write, including deadlines that prohibit putting it off and other priorities and interruptions. The right attitude here involves two things:

● Do not let perfection be the enemy of the good; in other words, get as close as you can to your ideal way of operating, do not let problems make you see the whole thing as impossible and abandon your good intentions entirely.
● Use habit to build up greater writing strength; for instance persevering with something until you *make it work for you*. For example, I used to be rather poor at writing on the move, but a busy life and regular travel made it necessary. Nowadays, after some perseverance, I can switch out the hustle and bustle of, say, a busy airport and get a good deal done.

In addition, you need to ensure the flow of your message so that it is well designed to progressively create a *persuasive* message as it is read; there is more about this in the next section.

Overall, the key to being persuasive is to see what needs to be done in the right light. Whatever *you* may want, the focus must be on the other person and what will persuade them. Whoever they are – prospects or past customers – they make decisions in the same kind of way: they weigh up the pros and cons. If you make a good case, then they will perceive the advantages of agreeing with you as outweighing not doing so. You have to make a case to them in their terms. You must put matters over to them clearly and in a logical manner: the logic describing what may be the many and various advantages of them taking a particular action, while at the same time addressing and minimizing anything they may see as a snag.

It is not a process to be underestimated. It needs care and preparation, and often there may be a great deal hanging on what happens: if direct mail is a major part of your promotional mix then much of your revenue may be influenced, and even potentially small amounts are significant – who would want to lose even 10 per cent of their profit by inattention to detail?

From here on as you read it may help to collect and have by you some mailshots that have been addressed to you – both ones you like and ones you don't. What follows may help demonstrate why they succeeded or why they failed to have any impact on you. They can provide useful examples as you read.

Summary

The message here is simple: first, make what you say clear, make it persuasive and focus it on customer needs rather than on your view of the product. Secondly, take time and care to get the message right:

- Make the time: when and in what form allows your best writing?
- Go about the task of writing systematically.
- Create and work to a writing plan.
- Separate deciding *what* you are going to include (content) from *how* you are going to put it (style).
- Fix on an approach that suits you and stick with it, creating positive individual writing habits in the process.
- Give the task space and priority.
- Check, check and cheque [sic] again.

SUNDAY

MONDAY

TUESDAY

WEDNESDAY

THURSDAY

FRIDAY

SATURDAY

Fact check (answers at the back)

1. Which best describes what objectives should be?
   a) Unnecessary ❑
   b) Specifically defined ❑
   c) Stated in general terms ❑
   d) Undefined ❑

2. How should the response you want be pitched?
   a) What's easiest internally ❑
   b) What competitors do ❑
   c) What customers are likely to find most appropriate ❑
   d) It does not need stating ❑

3. In your copy, which of the following words is most important?
   a) We ❑
   b) Us ❑
   c) Them ❑
   d) You ❑

4. In your product/service description, which should predominate?
   a) Benefits ❑
   b) Features ❑
   c) Facts ❑
   d) Opinions ❑

5. Proof of claims is best offered by whom?
   a) You ❑
   b) Your colleagues ❑
   c) Competitors ❑
   d) Others than you ❑

6. How is writing copy best done?
   a) Hastily ❑
   b) Very slowly ❑
   c) With a careful and systematic approach ❑
   d) To a set formula ❑

7. How should you check your writing?
   a) Do it right and no checking is necessary ❑
   b) By delegating it ❑
   c) *Very* carefully and more than once ❑
   d) With just a quick glance ❑

8. How is writing best done?
   a) Fitted in with other things ❑
   b) In fits and starts ❑
   c) In the early morning ❑
   d) Uninterrupted and with concentration ❑

9. How is editing best done?
   a) After time to sleep on it ❑
   b) Immediately after writing ❑
   c) It should not be necessary ❑
   d) Late at night ❑

TUESDAY

The component mix

Deciding and writing the message you send out is vital and a good deal was said about this in the last chapter. But one element was ignored. That is the fact that the message is spread around, and to a degree repeated, in a number of different places. These can vary, but four are most often in evidence:

- a letter
- a brochure of some sort
- a reply vehicle (a card to send back, for instance)
- an envelope (or wrapper).

The success of the total message is not just dependent on how it is written, but how it appears in total across the shot. Today we examine these components in turn and also investigate factors important to organizing the whole shot.

What is sent out is put together from essentially four elements: brochures or leaflets, a covering letter, a reply facility and, of course, an envelope. While the envelope is always necessary (unless you use postcards or wrap your shot in plastic, though this too can carry a message), the other components can be varied. A 'shot' might consist only of a letter, or only of a brochure, or of a brochure that incorporates a reply coupon; or it might be more elaborate – a letter plus two or three brochures and a reply form and a return envelope. Clearly, many permutations are possible.

 Together the package must carry the total message and that message must be sufficiently persuasive to prompt action from a number of recipients, numerous enough to make the whole exercise profitable.

The word 'mailshot' implies one such mailing, while a 'campaign' implies a number of shots over time which may be about different elements of the range, each being separate, except that they are clearly from the same source. Alternatively, shots may be closer together and linked, meaning one message is stretched across, say, two separate entities, so that repetition reinforces the impact.

Next we look at the basic considerations regarding each element (we look at the process of putting the promotion together creatively later, and will revisit some of these elements).

In every case a range of possible approaches, styles and details are identified. Any mailshot using them all would simply sink under the profusion of its own gimmicks and become self-defeating. Each technique does have its place, however, and, carefully orchestrated, various combinations can be very effective. It is perhaps important not to take a censorious line in considering them. Of course, there are dangers of inappropriate approaches, but bear your customer in mind and remember that what one person finds pushy another finds persuasive; what one finds crass another finds fun or interesting. What matters ultimately is what causes a satisfactory response and nothing that does so in a way customers find acceptable should be overlooked. Remember, also, that the many detailed factors involved throughout the package build up a number of points, which individually seem of little significance, but may together increase the response rate noticeably. That said, let us start by taking a look at what the recipient sees first.

The envelope

This must be serviceable. This sounds obvious, but if there are a number of enclosures the envelope must get them to their destination unscathed. Some feel quality directly affects response rates, believing that a white envelope is better than a manila one. Like many of the possible permutations that are being reviewed, this can be tested.

An 'If undelivered return to address' message should sensibly be included. This will help to avoid waste and prompt updates to the list by identifying when things are wrongly addressed, people have gone away and so on.

Of course, some business recipients will not see the envelopes, as their secretaries or central administration will open the mail. But some will and some intermediaries will clip an informative envelope to the contents before passing it on. So you may consider having the first part of the message printed on the envelope. The purpose of the envelopes carrying such a message is not so much to help ensure they are opened (research actually shows that most are), it is more to influence the frame of mind in which they are opened, aiming to generate some, albeit small, interest even at this early stage. If such a message is appropriate, it may be complete in itself ('Details enclosed of how to reduce your tax bill') or questioning ('Do you want to pay less tax?') or leave more to be explained by the contents ('A way to save money ... details inside').

A technique that some swear increases response rates is to use an actual stamp rather than franking the postage; perhaps an idea to bear in mind when the number mailed is small and the potential business is high value.

Other devices are possible. For example, a window envelope may show a glimpse of the contents, colour may add to the effect and reflect a (perhaps recognizable) corporate colour used inside. Important though the envelope may be, it is what is inside that really generates the response. Post Office regulations specify how much and what form of printing is allowed on the envelope. Indeed, current postal regulations are quite complex, involving size, weight and more.

Check, in advance, whether what you plan falls foul of any such postal regulations before you go too far; it is not the moment to find that adjusting size slightly could have reduced the postage rate just after printing thousands of brochures.

Brochures and leaflets

These may be items used elsewhere, brochures salespeople distribute or leaflets you display in reception or at exhibitions. There is, however, no reason why such material should be suitable and you may need to produce new material, tailored specifically to the job in hand.

In either case, the brochure is unlikely always to set out to tell people 'everything there is to know about the product or firm'; rather, it may prompt a desire for investigation, more information or discussion. Too much information can even have the reverse effect. One hotel, sending direct mail to attract conference business, found that the numbers of potential clients coming to inspect the hotel doubled when they replaced a short letter and glossy comprehensive brochure with a longer letter, no brochure and an invitation to inspect. The brochure simply got people saying 'I can see what it's like, no need to visit'.

The production of brochures generally is an area of increasing professionalism and great care is needed in defining the objective, creating the right message and making sure the brochure looks good and reflects the image that the organization intends to project as well as any corporate graphic style or colour. The days of the bland, general brochure, very similar to those of other firms, describing the chronological history of the firm and everything it does and intended to be used for everything, are surely past? What is needed now is the ability to match each objective in each particular area with something specifically designed for the job. This may mean producing separate brochures for each product. It may mean that any corporate brochure is a folder with separate inserts aimed at different target groups or different types of customer. It may mean a revised brochure every year. It may even mean a difference between the sort of brochure that is right to give a prospective customer after a preliminary meeting and the sort that is suitable to present to an intermediary who may have a role in, say, recommending you to others. It is very much 'horses for courses'.

For direct mail purposes the brochure or leaflet concerned must be specific to the objective set for the particular promotion. Brochures may need to be reasonably self-standing, after all they may get separated from the covering letter, but the total content – letter plus brochure – also needs to hang together, to produce a complete and integrated message.

Overall, what must be created is something that is accurately directed at a specific group, with a clear objective in mind and – above all – that is persuasive. This may seem basic; of course, promotional material is there to inform, but it must do so persuasively. That is the prime purpose. But this does not mean moving to something that is inappropriately strident (which might in any case be self-defeating), and it does mean putting a clear emphasis on customer need and benefits (what things do for people, rather than what they are). Essentially, a less introspective approach, better designed to its purpose, is the rule.

There are a few rules to be observed about brochures and those rules that one might define as made to be broken. This is because brochures must be *creatively* constructed to reflect the image of the firm graphically, differentiate it from its competitors and aim the chosen message directly at the target group addressed.

For brochures and their close relation, catalogues (essentially a brochure listing many products), there is danger in being too neat – research shows that they work best modelled on a magazine rather than a report. In other words, present a slew of sections, panels and headlines rather than one neat panel. It is a fine line between too busy and not busy enough; as ever, test what works for you.

The covering letter

This is a crucial element to get right and there are several factors to consider.

The right appearance

Basics first. It must look right. It must be attractively laid out, grammatically correct and well presented. If selling a service this is perhaps especially important, since it gives the impression that the letter has come from an efficient and reputable firm.

The letterhead itself is important to the image: up to date yet not 'over the top' is what should be aimed at and this is not easy. Subjective judgements are involved. Ultimately, it is a matter of opinion and in smaller firms this can sometimes mean too safe a compromise, which may dilute impact. Consider, too, whether your standard letterhead is right for direct mail purposes.

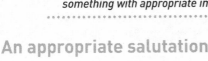

TIP *You might consider using a letterhead with the conventional corporate information and contact details at the bottom of the page, thus leaving the top for headlines, photos or something with appropriate impact.*

An appropriate salutation

The salutation is the next important item to consider. Numbers may preclude individual salutations. If you are not saying 'Dear Mr Smith', or 'Dear John', what do you say? One answer is nothing. Simply start with a heading. Doing so does not preclude you finishing with your name, though in this case you should omit 'Yours sincerely' and set the name close enough to the text so that it does not look as if the signature was forgotten, or matching the signature (or signatures) in order to give a personal touch. If you are only mailing small quantities then it is worth signing each letter.

On other occasions, a standardized opening may be necessary, for example:

- 'Dear Client or Customer' (that at least is clear)
- 'Dear Sir'
- 'Dear Reader'
- 'Dear Colleague'
- 'Dear Finance Director' (or other appropriate title), etc.

In many ways none of these is taken to be more than a token greeting and, unless it is something really novel, will have comparatively little impact. You should try to find a form of words you like, bearing in mind that perhaps almost anything is better than 'Dear Sir/Madam'!

TIP *Resist using internal descriptions as your salutation for different mailshots – the 'Dear Customer' shot may be fine, but on one famous occasion (reported in the press) a financial institution selling investments sent out a shot having failed to change the internal tag. It began 'Dear Rich Bastard ...' Bankers!*

The need for a structure

In selling face to face, you can adapt your approach to the individual you are with as the conversation proceeds. In a letter mailed in quantity this is not possible, and a formula to structure the approach is useful. The classic sales acronym, AIDA, prompts you to see the progressive stages of your message and seek to create:

Attention
Interest
Desire
Action

This works well in providing a structure for letters and represents accurately the job to be done in prompting a response.

How letters are read

Before looking at how such a structure helps the composition of the letter, consider for a moment what happens when it is received. People seldom read a letter immediately in the same sequence in which it was written. Their eyes flick from the sender's address to the ending, then to the greeting and the first sentence, skim to the last – and then, if the sender is lucky, back to the first sentence for a more careful reading of the whole letter. Research has been done showing a clear sequence, so the first sentence is an important element in 'holding' the reader and it should arouse immediate interest. Clichés abound and the list that follows shows the kind of approach to avoid; do not start with:

- 'We respectfully suggest ...'
- 'I have pleasure in enclosing ...'
- 'Referring to the attached ...'
- 'I would like to take this opportunity ...'
- 'Allow me to say ...'

With that in mind, consider the sequence of the letter, looking at it first as a whole. It will, I hope, be clear by now that the copy for the letter, as for the brochure(s) in fact, is crucial. You are unlikely to be able to dictate it straight away, certainly not to begin with.

A letter will need thinking about and planning and it will probably go through a number of drafts. Write down the key points, headings, identify the main benefits – create a skeleton. Then, with some guidelines in mind, you can look at how it all goes together.

Attention – the opening

The most important part of the letter is the start. It may well determine whether the rest of the letter is read. The opening may be quite short, a heading nearly always works best (and it can be a long one), then followed by a couple of sentences, or two paragraphs, but the whole beginning is always disproportionately important. A good start will help as you write the letter, as well as ensuring the recipient reads it. Omit or keep references short and make subject headings to the point – the reader's point. Do not use 'Re', it's old fashioned, over formal and unnecessary. Make sure the start of the letter will command attention, gain interest and lead easily into the main text. How do you do this? You could try the following:

- Ask a 'Yes' question (i.e. something you know will create a positive thought – *Do you want to save money?*).
- Explain why you are writing to that reader particularly.
- Explain why the reader should read the letter.
- Flatter the reader (carefully).
- Explain what might be lost if the reader ignores the message.
- Give the reader some 'mind-bending' news (if you have any).

Interest/desire – the body of the letter

The body of the letter runs straight on from the opening. It must consider the reader's needs or problems from their point of view. It must interest them. It must get them nodding in agreement: 'Yes, I wish you could help me with that.'

Of course (you say) you are able to help them. In drafting you must write what you intend for the readers and, of course, list the benefits you can offer (linked appropriately to features) and in particular the benefits which will help them solve their problems and satisfy their needs.

You have to anticipate the reader's possible objections to your proposition in order to select your strongest benefits and most convincing answers. If there is a need to counter objections, then you may need to make your letter longer and give proof, for example adding comment from a third party that the benefits are genuine. However, remember to keep the letter as short as possible, but still as long as necessary to complete the case. If that is two, three or more pages, so be it.

TIP *One way to keep people reading is to avoid being neat. When there is more than one page, make them turn over, not after a full stop, but in the middle of a sentence; they are more likely to read on than finish half way through a ... [sic].*

It is easy to find yourself quoting the literature that will accompany the letter to the reader. If you were writing a lecture on the subject, you would probably need all that information. When writing to a prospective customer you have to select just the key benefits which will be of particular value to the reader and which support the literature.

The body copy must:

● keep the reader's immediate interest
● develop that interest with the best benefit
● win the reader over with a second benefit and then further benefits.

The next job is to ensure action from the reader by a firm close.

Action – the letter ending

In closing you can make a (short) summary of the benefits of the proposition. Having decided on the action you want the reader to take, you must be positive about the merits (for them) of their taking it.

It is necessary to nudge the reader into action with a decisive close. Do not use phrases like these:

- 'We look forward to hearing ...'
- 'I trust you have given ...'
- '... favour of your instructions'
- '... doing business with you'
- 'I hope I can be of further assistance.'

All such phrases are really just padding between the last point and 'Yours sincerely'. Instead, use real closing phrases.

Alternative closes

Some alternative ways of closing your letter might include:

- Asking the reader to telephone or write.
- Suggesting they telephone or use the reply-paid envelope.
- Prompting them to ask for a meeting or more information.

We'll now look at some other alternative closes.

Immediate gain

This offers something in return for the recipient taking prompt action: for example, 'Return the card today and your profitability could be improved', or 'Send the order within seven days and get delivery post free'.

'Best' solution

This summarizes: 'You want a system that can cope with occasional off-peak demands, that is easy to operate by semi-skilled staff and is presented in a form that will encourage line managers to use it. The best fit with all these requirements is our system 'X'. Return the card indicating the best time to install it.'

Direct request

Examples might include:

- 'Post the card today'
- 'Telephone us without delay'

Signing off

Consider, too, the person who should have their name at the bottom of the letter. Replies will tend to come back to them and so will queries. So should it be the sales office, one director or another and how well are they able to cope with any response? Make sure their name is typed as well, as signatures tend to be awkward to read, and that a note of the position they hold in the firm is included. People like to know who they are dealing with.

Only use names that are available, i.e. do not create a situation where a senior person's name signs off the letter, but any enquirer asking for them on the telephone is passed on. I know one company where all sales letters are signed in a fictitious name and everyone fielding sales enquiries answers with that name! Hmm, I'm not sure, though it seems to work.

PS

Remember the power of the postscript. Tradition suggests that these are for things inadvertently left out (their use predates word processing and easy editing), while direct mailers will tell you they get read. Use them for repetition or to add emphasis, or a final benefit – doing so can strengthen the message.

PPS

Some people even use two!

Language

Finally, we should consider the language used in such letters. Many people have acquired a habit of artificiality in writing, approaching it quite differently from their way of talking to a customer and that can reduce their chances of making a sale through over-formality.

An appropriate tone

The language you use is clearly important. It must be clear, appropriate and have sufficient impact to persuade. The checklist below sets out some basic rules for persuasive copy.

- **Be clear.** Make sure that the message is straightforward and uncluttered by 'padding'. Use short words and phrases. Avoid (or explain) jargon.
- **Be natural.** Do not project yourself differently just because it is in writing.
- **Be positive.** In tone and emphasis (be helpful).
- **Be courteous.** Always.
- **Be efficient.** Project the right image.
- **Be personal.** Use 'I' rather than 'we' – say what *you* will do (while avoiding the inappropriate introspection referred to earlier).
- **Be appreciative.** 'Thank you' is a good phrase.

The next checklist examines specific aspects of the language used in letters. I hope this is not labouring the point, but some people in smaller businesses, who have no training in marketing but a strong background in, say, the technicalities of what they do, can have a tendency towards gobbledegook. I recently saw a note tabled at a board meeting on recommendations proposed by a broker about pension schemes. After a long silence someone said 'I don't understand it', immediately joined by a chorus of 'Neither do I'. This must not be the general reaction to the material contained in your direct mail.

- **Avoid pomposity.** Examples include:
  - 'We beg to advise ...'
  - 'The position with regard to ...'
  - 'It will be appreciated that ...'
  - 'It is suggested that the reasons ...'
  - 'The undersigned/writer ...'
  - 'May we take this opportunity of ...'
  - 'Allow me to say in this instance ...'

- 'Having regard to the fact that ...'
- 'We should point out that ...'
- 'Answering in the affirmative/negative ...'
- 'We are not in a position to ...'
- 'The opportunity is taken to mention ...'
- 'Dispatched under separate cover ...'

- **Avoid coldness and bad psychology that sounds hectoring or over-formal.** Therefore use:
  - *Inform* rather than *advise*
  - *Note* rather than *learn*
  - Positive phrases, e.g. do not *regret* what can't be done, stress what can be done and make it attractive.

- **Avoid cliché endings.** Examples are:
  - 'Thanking you in advance ...'
  - 'Assuring you of our best attention at all times, we remain ...'
  - 'Trusting we may be favoured with ...'
  - 'Awaiting a favourable reply ...'
  - 'Please do not hesitate to ...'

- **Keep it simple.** Prefer short words to long, for example:
  - *Approximately* becomes *about*
  - *Commencement* becomes *start*
  - *Elucidate* becomes *explain*
  - *Considerable* becomes *great*

- **Prefer one or two words to several.** Examples are:
  - *At this moment in time* becomes *now*
  - *Due to the fact that* becomes *because*
  - *In the not too distant future* becomes *soon*
  - *There can be no doubt about* becomes *it is certain*
  - *Should the situation arise* becomes *if*

Overall, aim for short sentences. In fact, a mix of longer and shorter sentences works well; the suggestion is not that every sentence should be only four words long. This paragraph illustrates this.

Ditto short paragraphs.

Aim for an overall effect that sounds right when read out loud. Try it. Get a colleague to read your draft to you. Amend it. Sleep on it. Get it read again. There is no shame in taking a few moments to get such an important piece of writing right.

Presentation

Finally, remember that the end product should be neatly presented, in a way that the reader finds convenient and readable. Do not overlay text with colours that obscure, and use an adequately sized font; remember that more than half your readers will wear spectacles. So, to ensure the finishing touches add impact you should think about the following:

- Position the letter on the page according to the amount of the text. It is unattractive if there is a huge expanse of white below a very short letter. Position it lower down, in that case, or consider having two sizes of letterhead paper printed and put short letters on the smaller sheets.
- 'Block' paragraphs, with double spacing between each paragraph for greater clarity and smartness.
- Leave at least 1½ inches (3 cm) at the foot of the page before going on to the second page; leave a bigger space to avoid having only one or two lines (plus farewells) on the second page.
- Allow enough space for the signature, name and job title. It is better to carry the letter over on to another page than cram it in at the bottom.
- Note, at the foot of the last page, the enclosures mentioned in the text and sent with the letter.

- Fold brochures sensibly and staple the pages of a multi-page letter together to avoid losses.
- Number the pages.
- Number the paragraphs when a lot of points have to be covered or use bullet points.
- Underline all headings or make them bold.

Remember, layout of this sort of material cannot simply go by default. The way a letter is to be presented must be considered and specified by the writer to ensure the final layout works.

Graphic emphasis can be made, in this age of word processing, in a number of ways, with:

CAPITALS
<u>Underlining</u>
  Indenting
Bold
Colour
Italics

While these features should not be overdone, they can be useful and, in whatever form and combination you select, need specifying to the typesetter/printer.

Remember that there is no reason why a letter cannot include illustrations (photographs, pictures, cartoons, graphs and more), though this means more work to ensure a pleasing and legible layout, and text should normally predominate. It is also good to make sure every illustration has a caption; readers must be clear why it is shown.

Make it easy to reply

Most mailings need some reply device. This may be a coupon, a form to be completed or a self-contained, reply-paid card. Whatever format you select, how it is to be used should be completely clear. It is fatal to have someone who is interested to the point of taking action being put off just because the way to reply seems unclear.

So make it clear. Decide what information you want. If you ask for a name and address, adding a request for their job title may make the follow-up just that little bit easier. Let them tick boxes rather than write essays. Let them send their business card rather than filling in anything.

Do not forget to include your telephone number, print it clearly and consider the freephone options, and certainly consider how to make it easy to get through. It is without doubt a courtesy to use reply-paid letters or cards (or freepost). If you opt for reply-paid, do make it first class, since there is something incongruous about asking for an urgent response and then offering a second-class envelope in which to send it back.

Allow enough time, since there are arrangements to be made and you will need to liaise with the Post Office. The standard reply-paid format seems straightforward, but requires a licence (thereafter you only pay for those that come back) and must conform to the prescribed format in terms of both size and style of printing.

Think carefully before you omit this element of the total package – an easy means of response can make all the difference to your results. And do not treat it as a simple extra – check it carefully and ask someone else if the description of *exactly* how responses should be made is clear and the method of returning it simple and appropriate.

Here is a further thought, at least for small, specialist shots. Research shows that actually putting a postage stamp on the reply envelope, rather than using a printed reply-paid format, can double your responses. Clearly it costs more, as you pay for all the reply envelopes you send out rather than only those that come back, but the resulting responses may be worth more in the long run.

Measuring results

Having touched on the reply vehicle, as this is primarily what provides feedback, it now seems appropriate to pause and consider the monitoring of direct mail activity. One of the advantages of direct mail is its ability to be tested and fine-tuned easily and at low cost.

The reply card can be coded either to the list (or portion of it) used, or the mailing material, or both. In other words, different versions of the mailing can be used and a check kept on how responses vary. If different batches of reply cards are produced with variations, they can be sorted and checked on receipt. The code may literally be a code, batches A and B (with A or B printed in the corner); or the return address may be varied, with responses addressed to say Department X or Y and so on. In this way, not only can immediate response be measured but, in the longer term, conversion rates can be checked too. It could be that, in monitoring two lists, you find that one produces twice as many initial responses, but the quality of prospect and conversion rate make it less effective. All such information helps you make future shots better.

In terms of the detail of the mailing, if split runs are used a variety of comparisons may be made. This can be well worth checking and you should never underestimate the difference minor changes – which you may even regard as cosmetic – can make.

.For example, you could check factors such as the following, one against another.

- **Copy.** For example, long versus short, punchy versus conversational
- **Colour**. One colour versus another, or black and white versus colour(s)
- **Reply vehicle.** Card versus form
- **Cost.** Reference to price versus no reference
- **Product/service.** Reference to one or more
- **Illustrations.** Include or not, and different types (e.g. photos or drawings)
- **Offering.** Here there will be many options that might be compared: from suggesting people just go straight to fixing a meeting or asking for more information in some way first, to attending an event or logging on to a website.

In fact, any variable element can be tested in this way continuously over time. Because this process inevitably makes for complications at origination and production stages, it is often neglected. The possible improvement of results that can be created as this kind of database builds up can, however, make the time and effort involved well worthwhile.

And what sort of results *can* you expect?

Response rates from direct mail vary enormously. In some fields companies make a good living from response rates of less than 1 per cent, while in others up to 50 per cent may be achieved (mailings to past – satisfied – customers for instance can produce high returns). It is only the relationship between money spent and the revenue generated that ultimately matters and on which success can be judged.

It is worth defining 'response' clearly. The percentage of those mailed responding is most usually the number focused on. But what this should be is, inherently, dependent on so many disparate factors as to create difficulty. That apart, what do you want to count as success? This might be orders, payments (remember the old saying that it's not an order until the money is in the bank!), or it might be enquiries, meetings arranged, samples sent out, links to your website activated, or more. Where stages are involved, each one can be measured: for instance the ratio of enquiries, sales meetings resulting and then orders placed.

You need to think about exactly what it makes best sense to measure and then concentrate as much on the profitability delivered as on the comparison with other methods, campaigns or even competitors (though information about them may only be hearsay and only act to confuse). After all, for one organization receiving a 2 per cent response may be excellent, but in other circumstances it could be disastrous. Other measures you might consider include:

- Total revenue received (even some time after the event)
- The number of new, first-time, customers
- The number of returning customers
- Average order value
- Orders/product mix
- The unit response cost (total mailing cost divided by the number responding)

- Individual contribution (the average order value minus the unit response cost)

Any of the above may be useful, as may other measures. Defining and measuring all interim stages may help you find more measures that are important to you – their relative usefulness will depend on the nature of your business. Certainly, only by monitoring these sorts of factor can you see how you are doing and ensure that your results are profitable and that they are maintained or improved rather than declining.

Timing and cost

Having reviewed the core elements of a shot and because there are a variety of elements that make up the total, let's turn to costs: it is essential to work out your costs carefully. Prepare a costing sheet, along the lines of the one shown opposite, so that you know in advance what will be involved.

 Never forget that the greatest cost may be time (yours and other people's) and this may need reflecting in your cost calculations too.

Do not forget those costs incurred after the material has been posted, and that prompt, efficient and effective action when a reply is received also costs money.

If you are a first-time direct mail user, talk to the Post Office, who have a number of attractive start-up schemes; these vary over time, but sometimes include cost-saving devices such as a scheme allowing you to send a certain quantity of mail post-free.

As well as keeping a close eye on, and a written note of, costs, the schedule of timings can also be usefully recorded in calendar style. Copy has to be written, brochures must be designed and printed, overprinted (rather than plain) envelopes need a longer lead time when ordered and, if you are contracting out the collation, insertion and posting this also needs a little time.

Costing sheet

Item	Cost	Cost per thousand
Brochure: Copy		
Design		
Printing		
Letter: Copy/design		
Printing		
Envelopes/wrapping		
Reply mechanism: Design		
Print		
Reply paid cost (estimate)		
Mailing: Collating		
Stapling/folding		
Insertion		
Postage (1st/2nd/rebated rate)		
Other enclosures: (how many?)		
Follow-up costs: (much could be included here, from sales meetings to events)		
Miscellanies		
TOTAL		

And so on. If you are working back from a planned arrival date – perhaps you want this to be exactly four weeks before a planned event – even the time spent in the post needs estimating.

Always circulate material internally well ahead of posting, together with any briefing and a special note to those who will be involved in response action once replies start to arrive. It gives the wrong impression if recipients telephone saying they want more information about something they have seen in a mailshot and the switchboard (or, worse still, a senior member of staff) can only say 'What mailshot?' Such own goals must be avoided or the impact is diluted and possible new business may go by default.

Summary

If any chapter in this book spells out the truth that direct mail's success is a question of detail, it is this one. Each and every component of the shot needs care and attention to get it working as best it can. In originating your shots it is worth noting all the proven techniques that seem to make things work more effectively, and testing alternatives before you settle on one main way forward (though ongoing promotion needs to be regularly reviewed – letting it repeat automatically risks diluting effectiveness over time). The message here is a positive one: attention to detail pays dividends and gets the best results; though the origination of everything involved needs to be creative – and there is more about that in the next chapter.

SUNDAY
MONDAY
TUESDAY
WEDNESDAY
THURSDAY
FRIDAY
SATURDAY

Fact check (answers at the back)

1. What's the primary purpose of an envelope (other than to contain the contents)?
   a) It's of no relevance ❑
   b) To carry the return address ❑
   c) To add colour ❑
   d) To influence the recipient's mood ❑

2. How should a brochure and a letter relate?
   a) The contents of one should duplicate the other ❑
   b) The contents of each should complement the other ❑
   c) They should not appear to go together ❑
   d) One should be words, the other pictures ❑

3. How should you view the letter's salutation?
   a) It must be carefully and appropriately chosen ❑
   b) It should always be 'Dear Sir/Madam to encompass all ❑
   c) Anything will do ❑
   d) It should be printed in red ❑

4. What is the most important part of the letter?
   a) All of it ❑
   b) The start ❑
   c) The middle ❑
   d) The fourth sentence ❑

5. How do you best specify the action you want recipients to take?
   a) Leave the recipient to decide ❑
   b) Don't mention it at all ❑
   c) Insist on only one action ❑
   d) Specify exactly and provide a choice ❑

6. Why should you consider using a PS on a letter?
   a) It looks clever ❑
   b) To accommodate text you forget earlier ❑
   c) It is proven to be well read and can add emphasis ❑
   d) It's expected ❑

7. Which of the following is it most important to be when you make your shot?
   a) Clever ❑
   b) Creative ❑
   c) Clear ❑
   d) Controversial ❑

8. Which of the following reads most easily?
   a) At this moment in time ❑
   b) Now ❑
   c) At the present moment ❑
   d) At this precise minute ❑

9. How much should you use graphic emphasis (**bold type, CAPITALS** etc.)?
   a) As much as possible ❑
   b) Every second line ❑
   c) When appropriate to emphasize a key point ❑
   d) Not at all ❑

10. When you should test your approaches?
    a) Never ❑
    b) The first time used ❑
    c) Annually ❑
    d) On a systematic basis linked to changes made ❑

WEDNESDAY

Creatively enhancing persuasiveness

Creativity is more than making things effective: it aims to make things look different, striking and memorable. Perhaps in the context of direct mail and in many product areas, it is about making things, which are essentially similar, appear different.

Taking a creative approach is how you turn something from routine into special and how you act to prompt potential customers to go beyond just taking an interest – to taking action, to buy.

There can be no magic formula either for 'being creative' or, much less, for creating the 'perfect' direct mail promotion. By definition it involves seeking new approaches, rather than slavishly following a format. This could imply a clever and striking idea, such as the company selling packing material (the sort of foam in which the shape of, say, a camera is cut out) who sent a mailshot with a box containing a raw hen's egg as a way of demonstrating their product's protective qualities. A clever idea, and one that worked because it was not a gimmick but wholly relevant.

But creativity must infect every part of the process; one overriding clever idea is never sufficient alone. With that in mind, this chapter sets out some principles and floats some ideas. But it is essentially concerned with prompting an approach that will focus the thinking in the right way, allow you to devise approaches that will create interest and give you an edge on your competition, rather than 'script' things for you.

TIP *Look at the ideas in this chapter, and also observe good ideas in other people's promotion. Sometimes you can usefully copy the ideas of others (though not too slavishly); more often you can use one idea to spark another and what you come up with will really give your shot an edge.*

Definition of the brief

The overall intention

First make some notes and start by reviewing the whole promotional message rather than one component, such as the letter, and get absolutely straight in your mind what the overall message is to be. Ask yourself particularly how what you have to say is new, unique or at least different from the way others may present themselves. To whom exactly is it aimed? And is this a sufficiently discrete group? If you try to appeal to too broad a spectrum of recipients at once, you may end up not interesting any of them because your message is not sufficiently specific. Clearly rather different approaches, even a different tone, will be necessary for existing customers and others.

You must decide whether you are presenting the organization, a product range, or particular aspects of either, and if it is the latter what aspects you will pick. Is the message of topical relevance? Can you describe it in terms of advantages and benefits and if it includes service can you describe exactly what this means? What are you going to say about costs? What about value for money? What guarantees, proof and testimonials can you offer? And, bearing in mind that the route to action is also important, how can you make the asked-for action easy and attractive?

Put this down on paper in note form, not aiming for final copy, and try to think objectively about how it will appeal. Is it in the best possible approach? Would it interest *you*? In addition, you need to think of some *additional* factors to give greater power to how your case will be explained and presented.

Using 'hooks'

What are hooks? They are a variety of elements that will generate the interest you want by focusing attention in a particular way. Here are some examples:

- **Combinations.** Featuring two things linked together, e.g. a budget analysis and action plan (for an accountant) or a computer and printer.
- **Team.** Something to be responded to by more than one person, e.g. a meeting designed for the managing director and his finance director to attend together.
- **Limited offer.** 'Only a limited number can attend', 'Only limited stocks are available', 'This price until ...'
- **Status.** Offering people the opportunity to be the first with something, such as meeting at a prestige venue, where they might meet local opinion leaders.
- **A competition.** The prize may be the product or some element or sample of it; for example it might be something simple, like a bottle of Scotch, or more elaborate, like a holiday.
- **Sponsorship.** Link to an event, perhaps a charitable event, e.g. 'Meet us on such and such a date and join us at the local theatre club where we are sponsoring the production of ... in the evening'.

- **Highlight the source.** If you are using an external list you can opt to feature the list link itself, e.g. 'As a member of ... ', 'As an investor with ...'
- **Second chance.** Mail people a second time as a 'reminder' or to increase the appeal.

You can also highlight aspects of the overall message. Here are some examples:

- **Timing.** An offer that will give a benefit, for example 'before the holidays' or 'by the end of the (financial) year'.
- **Exclusivity.** An offer to a select group, e.g. 'Only for existing clients', 'Only for local business people', 'Only for farmers in Sussex'.
- **Straight reward.** An incentive, essentially something of value, on whatever scale (ranging from the insurance company that gives you a pen just for letting them quote to a more tangible reward given on purchase). Note that any such gifts need to have a wide appeal.

Such factors as these are clearly not mutually exclusive. They can be linked, added to and no doubt bettered. No one knows in advance what degree of gimmick will appeal, so be careful, but remember that the recipients will probably take a less censorious view than you of such matters. Some level of experiment may well prove worthwhile, although perhaps if you are not prepared to be a pioneer, keep a sharp eye on what is done by others.

Finally, keep in mind the key things people may want to obtain from your offering. These include people being able to:

- make more money
- save money
- save time, effort or hassle
- be more secure
- sort problems
- exploit opportunities
- motivate their staff
- impress their customers, friends or family
- persuade others more readily (their bank manager or shareholders).

Whatever applies, and I am sure you can add to this list, you will need to say so. And if the benefits include being able to do something more quickly, more easily, more cost-effectively or more anything else, say that too. If you believe you provide something of real value, have the courage of your convictions and say so. If reading your promotion does not clearly show the reader you believe in it, why ever should they do so?

With all this in mind you can begin to get some real copy down on paper. There are two key aspects to this: the words (the tone, language and approach you use) and the structure into which you fit the words to complete the message.

Writing powerful words

The actual (systematic) process of writing was discussed earlier. Here, the focus is on making it highly readable. The point about keeping it simple has already been made, but it is worth repeating here.

So, use short words and short sentences.

And short paragraphs.

Do not use too much jargon; at worst this will kill a message stone dead, at best it will dilute the message. If jargon must be used, then explain it the first time a description appears.

But, as Bernard Shaw, said, 'The golden rule is that there are no golden rules'. This means do nothing to excess. Sometimes you will need a longer word, a long sentence and some judiciously chosen jargon.

Two other approaches should pervade the text. First, remember that it should be written from the customer's, or a potential customer's, point of view.

 TIP *A good way to double-check that you are not being too introspective is to count the number of times the word 'you' appears; it should outweigh the number of times the words 'I', 'we' or 'the company' appear.*

Secondly, it is not enough for your text to be positive, stating that 'this is the case', or 'this will be what is done', and rarely saying things like 'I think ...', 'Probably ...' or 'Maybe ...'. Experienced direct mailers talk about *magic* words or at least words that inject a tone that should always be present and that enhance interest. Some of these magic words are shown below:

free	today	timely	trial	special
guarantee	win	respected	immediately	
new	easy	reliable	high	value
announcing	save	opportunity		
you	at once	low cost		
now	unique	fresh.		

You must not overuse these words or your message will become blatantly over the top, but do not neglect them either. Be careful, too, not to use words that are so overworked that they have come to mean virtually nothing; for example, now every gadget in the visible universe has been described as 'user friendly' – does it have any descriptive power left? I don't think so.

You must keep searching for ways of making your copy perform better. Again, the following guidelines are designed not only to float some examples, but also to show the approach you need to cultivate. They are reviewed in terms of dos and don'ts, with no apology for any occasional repetition.

The don'ts
Your message should *not*:

- **Be too clever.** It is the argument that should win the reader round, not your flowery phrases, elegant quotations or clever puns.
- **Be too complicated.** The point about simplicity has been made. It applies equally to the overall argument.
- **Be pompous.** This means saying too much about you, your organization and your product/services (instead of what it means to the reader). It means writing in a way that is too far removed from the way you would speak. It means following too slavishly exact grammar at the expense of an easy, flowing style
- **Overclaim.** While you should certainly have the courage of your convictions, too many superlatives can become self-defeating. Make one claim that seems doubtful and the whole argument suffers.
- **Offer opinions.** At least, don't have too many compared with the statement of facts – ideally, substantiated facts.
- **Lead into points with negatives.** For example, do not say 'If this is not the case we will ...'; say rather 'You will find ... or ... '.
- **Assume your reader lacks knowledge.** Rather than saying, for example, 'You probably do not know that ...', it is better to say, 'Many people have not yet heard ...', or, 'Like others, you probably know ...'.
- **Overdo humour.** Never use humour unless you are very sure of it. An inward groan as they read does rather destroy the nodding agreement you are trying to build. A quotation or quip, particularly if it is relevant, is safer and even if the humour is not appreciated, the appropriateness may be noted.
- **Use up benefits early.** A direct mail letter must not run out of steam: it must end on a high note and still be talking in terms of benefits even towards and at the end.

The dos

You should *do* the following:

- **Concentrate on facts.** The case you put over must be credible and factual. And note that a clear-cut 'these are all the facts you need to know' approach tends to pay particular dividends when selling intangible services.
- **Use captions.** While pictures, illustrations, photographs and charts can often be regarded as speaking for themselves, they will have more impact if used with a caption. (This can be a good way of achieving acceptable repetition, with a mention in the text and in the caption.)
- **Use repetition.** Key points can appear more than once, for example in a leaflet and a letter, and even more than once within the letter itself. This applies, of course, especially to benefits repeated for emphasis.
- **Keep changing the language.** Get yourself a thesaurus. You need to find a number of different ways of saying the same thing in brochures and letters and so on.
- **Say what is new.** Assuming you have something new, novel – even unique – to say, make sure the reader knows it. Real differentiation can often be lost, so in the quantity of words make sure that the key points still stand out.
- **Address the recipient.** You must do this accurately and precisely. You must know exactly to whom you are writing, what their needs, likes and dislikes are and be ever conscious of tailoring the message. Going too far towards being all things to all people will dilute the effectiveness to any one recipient.
- **Keep them reading.** Consider breaking sentences at the end of a page so that readers have to turn over to complete the sentence. (Yes, it does not look quite so nice, but it works.) Always make it clear that other pages follow, putting 'continued ...' or similar at the foot of the page.
- **Link paragraphs.** This is another way to keep them reading. Use 'horse and cart' points to carry the argument along. For example, one paragraph starts 'One example of this is ...'; the next starts 'Now let's look at how that works ...'
- **Be descriptive – really descriptive.** For example, a system may be better described using the words 'smooth as silk'

rather than 'very straightforward to operate'. Or perhaps you need both sorts of phrase, the second spelling out your message in more detail. Remember, *you* know how good what you are describing is; the readers do not. You need to tell them and you must not assume they will catch your enthusiasm from a brief phrase.

● **Involve people.** First, involve your people. Do not say, 'The head of our XYZ Division', say, 'John Smith, the head of our XYZ Division'. And then involve other people. Do not say, 'It is a proven service ...', say, 'More than 300/3,000 clients have found it valuable ...'.

● **Add credibility.** For example, if you quote users, quote names (with their permission); if you quote figures, quote them specifically and mention people by name. Being specific adds to credibility, so do not say, 'This is described in our booklet on ...', but rather, 'This is described on page 16 of our booklet on ...'.

● **Use repetition.** Key points can appear more than once, in the leaflet and the letter, and even more than once within the letter itself. This applies, of course, especially to benefits repeated for emphasis. You will notice this paragraph is repeated, either to show that the technique works or perhaps to demonstrate that half-hearted attempts at humour are not altogether recommended.

If you have the habit of using things you shouldn't or forgetting good techniques that you want to use, then you can do no better than to make a personalized dos/don'ts list and keep it to hand.

Editing

A final comment in this section concerns editing – edit, edit, edit (more repetition). It is usually easier to start with more copy than you need and edit it back to the correct length, improving it as you go, rather than adding to a short draft (though with experience your writing will get closer and closer to the length you intend). In addition, it may need going over more than once and time spent in fine-tuning is often worthwhile.

Large- and small-scale promotion

To investigate this promotional method further we will consider two examples, both linked to the world of books. The first example is a flyer promoting a single book, designed to be used in various ways, for example mailed with a book cover or other items. The second example is promoting the benefits of buying a subscription and is a more complicated message.

Example 1: One book

Not all the books I have written are business ones and the book described below, *Empty When Half Full* (subtitled *A Cantankerous Consumer's Compilation of Mistakes, Misprints and Misinformation*), is essentially a rant against poor communication. One reviewer described it as 'hilarious', and whatever other publicity there was for it (and this was organized primarily through the publishers), I wanted to be sure my own clients and contacts knew about it and, more specifically, that they were prompted to purchase a copy.

NEW ... NEW ... NEW

Don't read this book on public transport!

If you don't want to be reduced to a sniggering mess in public, read my new book, *Empty When Half Full - A Cantankerous Consumer's Compilation of Mistakes, Misprints and Misinformation* in the privacy of your own home. It can't fail to make you laugh out loud, with its incredible collection of gaffes, misprints and downright deviousness found in instructions, notices, marketing and advertising messages.

No area is exempt from a forensic eye for imprecise, incorrect or dishonest writing, from multi-national companies and government bodies to prestigious publications. Examples from the book of the real life booboos range from the unfortunate: *'This manual has been carefully to remove any errors'* to the idiotic *'Blackcurrant juice comes in two flavours – orange and strawberry'*, *'Scandinavian slippers – buy one get one free'* to the infuriating *'The Adobe Updater must update itself before it can check for updates. Would you like to update Adobe Updater now?'* to the downright scary *'Passengers must stay with their luggage at all times or they will be taken away and destroyed.'*

Empty When Half Full has been likened to Lynne Truss's international best seller, *Eats, Shoots and Leaves*, in its humorous analysis of ungrammatical, poorly punctuated, sometimes surreal writing on labels, signs, instructions and advertising. But there are lessons here too and comment on the serious aspect of poor communication that highlights genuine dangers to consumers.

Some of the mistakes quoted could have potentially serious repercussions, but they are chosen primarily for their nonsensical quality and tendency to make us smile; perhaps we should rejoice that they made customers chuckle as they read the material from product providers produced with less care than we – or they – might wish.

'This is a must-read' suggests David Horchover FCIM, author of *Sales Promotion*. 'Great and avoidable gaffes in marketing and sales promotion are humorously exposed and lampooned by Forsyth's needle-sharp and witty observations.'

ORDER: *Launch offer*: copies are £9.99 each, currently £8.99 for a signed copy sent by return *post free*. Cheques should be made out to Patrick Forsyth and sent to the above address; or make contact via

www.patrickforsyth.com

The letter shown (albeit it in a reduced size) above was sent from my office together with a small flyer containing an order form. This was mailed just as the book was published and when a certain amount of other publicity was in evidence. It worked well. Of those receiving the letter more than 25 per cent ordered and, indeed, I suspect it may have influenced a number of later orders too. The overall numbers may have been modest, but this is very typical of one sort of use of direct mail that is ideal for small businesses. A series of such shots, each focusing on a different product or service, possibly using a series of lists, can be organized progressively throughout the year. In this way the set-up is manageable and a steady flow of orders may result. (Incidentally, *Empty When Half Full* is still available; I'll even extend the launch price to readers of this book!)

A further point is relevant here: do not be misled by percentages (you never saw a cheque made out with one on!). The numbers that make such promotion viable are not difficult to calculate and many organizations make a good living from responses of only 1 to 2 per cent, or sometimes less. In a sense this illustrates the wastefulness of direct mail, but what proportion of people turn a page and ignore a magazine advertisement? It is the nature of the beast and what matters is cost-effectiveness. The figures in this example may not, however, be totally untypical. If you are selling something new, to existing (key) contacts, you would expect a good response rate.

Even this small-scale example illustrates a number of points, which may be of general value. The message:

- was sent on a smart letterhead (not reproduced here)
- was personalized and addressed to individuals by name
- used simple word processing to achieve graphic emphasis, without overdoing it. A selective use of the following will always have greater impact than a solid page of standard text: headings, indentations, capital letters, underlining, bold/italic type, quotations and more (including a (colour) illustration – in this case the book's cover)

- offered a (very) small incentive, that of a small discount and free postage. Such an incentive need not be dramatic but is psychologically pleasing (everyone loves a bargain); it can also add to the urgency, being a reason, or perhaps another reason, to order *now*.
- used a style of language clearly directed at known contacts – style should always relate appropriately to the kind of people you are writing to and the relationship that exists (or which it is hoped to prompt).

While this is not offered as a perfect example – I am sure there could have been a dozen other ways of going about it – it was used and it worked well.

Example 2: Many books

Now let's look at something a little more elaborate (and apologies: the format of this book does not do full justice to what was originally sent, but is still a useful illustration).

The *Good Book Guide* is a publication of news and reviews about books linked to a postal ordering service. It is available on subscription (though the cost can be recouped in book orders) and is *not* a book club: there is no commitment to order.

Past promotion has been based on research (an understanding of what needs it aimed to satisfy). For example, the requirements of a UK subscriber are very different to those of an overseas subscriber and so the offer is positioned differently for each market; the overseas subscriber is desperate to get hold of English books at a reasonable price, whereas the UK subscriber may have a good local bookshop (and access to the Internet) but likes and needs advice about the best books on offer. Promotion must explain exactly what the product is to those who do not know it (it is available only on subscription, so is not visible on magazine racks); after all, a subscription asks for money up front for something people may previously never have heard of. The producers have used many direct mail techniques, including incentives (a discount and a book token), and a punchy style of writing – one that succeeds in presenting an exclusive, club-like feeling about subscribers.

10 great reasons
why you should subscribe to
The Good Book Guide today ...
(There are many more, but we don't have room to show you here!)

1 **Save up to 35% with our best-ever subscription offer**
Subscribe today to take advantage of an offer that can save you up to £53.
That's three FREE copies in your first year.

2 **We review the best new books**
Our lively magazine is published 12 times a year and offers insightful and
discerning reviews of more than 300 titles in each issue. We find the very
best from the many thousands of books published each year.

3 **Plus new DVDs and old favourites**
From feature films and dramas to comedy classics, we select the cream
of the new releases and the pick of the old favourites.

4 **We're independent and selective**
Our expert reviewers read literally hundreds of titles each month in
search of the best. Their concise, considered opinions will enable you to
make your own informed reading choices. You'll never miss a good book
again, nor will you have to waste time looking for them.

5 **ANY book, ANY time, ANY where**
We can obtain any title in print in the UK today. That's access to millions of
titles. Just let us know what you're after and our dedicated team will hunt
down the titles for you. You'll receive a swift, personal reply. It's all part of the
GBG service.

6 **A £10 Book Token, absolutely free**
Take advantage of this exclusive offer and claim your £10 Book Token
absolutely free. You can use this token against any recommended titles
you wish to order from us.

7 **Dedicated customer service**
Unlike many other companies today, we have real people ready to help with
any request or query you may have. For over 30 years we have been getting
the books you want, where you want them, when you want them. Just put
us to the test.

8 **Easy ordering at your convenience**
You can contact us by phone, fax, email or online. The choice is yours.

9 **Gift service and special offers**
Order any book to be sent as a gift, anywhere in the world. There's no
better way to send presents to friends around the world.

10 **No-quibble guarantee**
If for any reason you are not happy with any title we recommend, simply
return it and you will receive a full refund, no questions asked.

A variety of components have been used over the years: letters, facsimiles of pages of the *Guide*, accompanying brochures, special offers and more. The format of such things is impossible to reproduce clearly in a small-format book such as this, but the two exhibits that follow are both good examples of effective direct mail practice and act to flesh out what is being said here.

The first is a list of 'reasons to buy' (and buy now). I think this is well done and compiling such a list is a useful exercise for anyone creating a shot, whether it then appears verbatim or just influences your text. This is shown here incorporating elements of graphic emphasis (capital letters, etc.); the original appeared as the left-hand column on a two-column page with a small illustration of a token alongside point 6.

Such a list spells out an attractive offer. In this example it makes everything clear and is a good and effective part of the total pitch. The guarantee element is included at the end of this list and the fit with this and other elements of the promotion is consistent. Of course, it is easier to describe a good product than a poor one – and I believe this is a good one – and the elements can be varied (by the time you read this book, do not be surprised if some elements of the offer have changed).

The *Guide* has also mailed specific offers and one such is reproduced below. Again, this must be seen as part of a total, more complicated, shot (and is necessarily reduced a little in size here).

This kind of approach has a distinct flavour of what is called *mass exclusivity*, which is a useful concept for some products/ services. The phrase, mass exclusivity, which at first sight might appear inherently contradictory, was coined to describe a promotional approach which makes what is sold, or supplied – or both – appear exclusive, while making sure that large numbers of people see it that way. It is an approach which can be enhanced in (good) direct mail and is favoured by some who regularly promote a changing range of goods to the same customer. In the UK, catalogue promotions of companies like Rohan (idiosyncratic leisure/activity clothes) and Bibliophile

(who sell discounted books in a newsletter punctuated by chatty remarks and humorous quotations) are examples of this approach.

For a small firm, which by definition will sell to a manageable number of people, such an approach can work well; it is always worth considering and developing an appropriate style and very often building on it consistently rather than making every new promotion completely different.

Simple ... but effective

Having looked at an example, albeit a cost-effective one, which involved a number of elements (a two-page letter, enclosures, reply-paid envelope and – in the message – incentives), let us not forget how useful simple reminders may be. For example, mailing:

- a postcard (used effectively, but not exclusively, by holiday companies such as hotels and travel agents)
- a Christmas card (or other seasonal reminder, including anniversaries of purchase, of your organization)

- a copy of some other promotion (a copy to customers of a press clipping or a printout of a forthcoming advertisement)
- an invitation card (to an event or just using the style)
- a reminder card for a specific time (a car due to be serviced, a dental appointment)
- a message designed to fit a Filofax (or organizer/diary system)
- a card or poster designed to go on a notice board, perhaps mailed to a company as an offer to staff (nearby hairdresser, restaurant) or just tailored to the place (a typing service, situated near a university, offering to produce student theses)
- a message on a sticky-backed (often yellow) note
- a copy of a press release
- a testimonial
- a label to stick to the telephone, reminding people of your number
- a sticker to serve as a reminder in a specific relevant place (a cartridge supplier on a printer, for instance); some have magnetic backs.

Such approaches, with or without some incentive (samples, a trial offer coupon or whatever) work well. Some of these examples need not be posted separately; they can be distributed with the product in the way a card allowing you to request a catalogue may be slipped by a publisher into the books they sell (or, indeed, by the bookseller – as most packages from Amazon contain a plug for some potential future purchase).

You need to keep ringing the changes. One hotel manager has kept in touch with me for almost 20 years. He has moved hotel, company and country a number of times, but about every six months something comes through the post from him. He uses a number of simple ideas as listed above – some have been repeated in different forms – but they have maintained awareness and business has resulted (otherwise I would no doubt eventually have been deleted from the list). Finally, as this example also makes clear, you need to be *systematic* and *persistent*. Building these elements into your direct mail need not be costly, but it pays dividends.

Summary

Two things are important to making your shots creative. The first is a question of the tried-and-tested devices like those mentioned in this chapter. These are not mutually exclusive and can be used in a variety of ways and in a variety of combinations. But, secondly, exactly *how* they are used is open to creative enhancement. For instance, it is well established that the envelope is important and I must have received so many over the years, but only one was tied across with string and sealed with old-fashioned sealing wax. I remember there being no way I was not going to open it and see what sort of organization was using such a device.

The good thing about creativity is that there are so many possibilities; if you want to make your shot memorable, you will find a way.

SUNDAY
MONDAY
TUESDAY
WEDNESDAY
THURSDAY
FRIDAY
SATURDAY

Fact check (answers at the back)

1. Which of these is a simple, low-cost method of direct mail?
   a) Twenty-page catalogue ☐
   b) Ten-page letter ☐
   c) Postcard ☐
   d) Twelve separate inserts ☐

2. At whom should a shot be aimed?
   a) The world and his wife ☐
   b) A well-identified and defined group ☐
   c) Whoever lives at number 10 Acacia Avenue ☐
   d) Recipients' pets ☐

3. What is a 'hook' intended to do?
   a) Make a mailshot look clever ☐
   b) Catch fish ☐
   c) Increase interest, readership and response ☐
   d) Make readers uncomfortable ☐

4. How should editing your copy be done?
   a) It should not be needed ☐
   b) As a final check ☐
   c) *Very* carefully ☐
   d) Hastily so as not to waste time ☐

5. Which of the following is a so-called 'magic' word?
   a) Dry ☐
   b) New ☐
   c) Costly ☐
   d) Message ☐

6. What should an over-complex message be?
   a) Avoided ☐
   b) Used ☐
   c) Made more complex still ☐
   d) Made humorous ☐

7. Any humour used needs to be what?
   a) Rude ☐
   b) Risqué ☐
   c) Carefully considered ☐
   d) Groan inducing ☐

8. Which technique helps keep people reading?
   a) Cat and dog ☐
   b) Mustard and cress ☐
   c) Horse and cart ☐
   d) Beer and skittles ☐

9. How should you refer to your team?
   a) By name ☐
   b) Not at all ☐
   c) By their function ☐
   d) By describing their appearance ☐

THURSDAY

Follow-up activity

Let's be positive; let's assume that a recent mailshot is working, replies are coming in and you need to handle these (whether enquiries or orders) in a way that maximizes the chances of repeat and ongoing business. And, not least, that means doing so efficiently.

In this chapter you will find some suggestions about follow-up, in three areas:

1 when you need more than one input to secure the response
2 when you receive a response
3 when you need to maintain contact in the longer term to manage the relationship, maintain customers' recall of you and prompt ongoing business.

Repetition

Customers face uncountable promotional hits: advertising and promotion in all its forms throughout the day, and the night too, for that matter. It is best not to overestimate their recall of you. Even if their experience of you is good, and this may range from just seeing messages from you or about you to enquiring or purchasing and being well satisfied with the way you operate, their memory of you will fade.

This is why repetition is so important, and it's why you see the same advertisements repeated so much on television; it's expensive, but repetition works. Multiple shots is one technique that fits here, and we should differentiate between what we might call 'linked shots' and 'linking shots'.

Linked shots

By this I mean that the 'shot' is in fact in two or more parts, the total message is designed to be spread and to have added impact because of the double (or multiple) hit. This can take a variety of forms: for example a 'teaser' first shot that gives little information, perhaps about something new, but is designed to intrigue, almost to whet the appetite for the next. It can also contain a facility to register interest and be kept informed (as a priority contact); this is a process that builds your list and identifies good prospects. This is then followed, days or weeks later, by another shot explaining fully and with the facility to reply. The dual nature is evident in the message, with the two entities creating a total hit and this being apparent to the recipient.

Linking shots

This phrase describes numbers of shots that simply create a continuity of message over time (and this could be years). There are some companies that mail us regularly. If we are not interested then we throw them out or take steps to get off the list. If we are interested then we will look at things and if we continue to buy occasionally or regularly we will be kept on the list. Thus a clothes company might mail something several times a year on a timing linked to the seasons, new products launched, when their sale time is and so on.

With campaigns of this sort, one shot and the next can be either of the following:

- **Essentially separate.** Each shot will make complete sense to someone who is receiving something from the organization for the first time.
- **Building continuity.** In such a case there is a clear link between one shot and the next and sometimes, if past customers receive a shot that is different to those going to prospects, it can have an element of personalization; for instance, actually linking to information about the last order someone placed.

A wealth of possibilities exists here. Such shots may be more powerful, more effective, but they will also be more expensive (double the postage cost for a start) so this must be borne in mind as a campaign is originated and costed; this is especially true of linked shots.

Effective response

The second area to consider here is action needed when you get an interim response that is something less than an order. Interim responses must be dealt with promptly, efficiently and courteously. This means, among other things that:

- Phone enquiries must be promptly handled, and certainly not preceded by an annoying and time-consuming automated process of pushing options before an enquirer can speak to a real person; many will opt out of this.
- Any additional information sent must go to the enquirer promptly (using post, email or whatever is appropriate).
- Clear records should be kept and action planned to follow up further – for instance a mailshot might produce, say, a telephone enquiry; more information is sent and then, to

prompt the next logical step, which let's say is for a sales person to make a face-to-face visit, another phone call might need to be made to follow up.

MARY'S PHONE'S ALWAYS RINGING

TIP *It is always useful to make sure that everyone who has a role in customer contact sees and becomes familiar with direct mail material so that they can talk fluently to customers who may have a copy in front of them.*

System is involved here too and follow-up action needs to be arranged to be appropriate and cost-effective, and controls should be in place to make sure it happens. It is clearly a waste of time and money to take action that creates leads and then let things falter for lack of thought-through follow-up action.

A further consideration here is fulfilment and that too is a sales consideration. A customer may order happily and be content with the product you supply, but if it arrives late, has to be chased to get it dispatched or arrives damaged (or even nearly damaged: perhaps they just feel packing is inadequate), then any such dissatisfaction will come to mind when they hear from you or consider ordering again. Be warned: the best mailshots in the world will not win you continuing business if other aspects of the way your organization is managed and operates are seen as not up to expectations.

Customer management

The final thing to consider here is the question of keeping in touch with customers. Of course customers will go on your mailing list, but you also need to make other decisions and perhaps to take other action. For small businesses, where numbers are manageable, the degree of personalization can be considerable. Certainly you should consider such things as:

- Categorizing customers into sub-groups – this might be by size, location, nature, products bought, amount spent and more. For instance, you might want to mail offering customers of a certain size a deal linked to a retailer or distributor local to them.
- Adding to the frequency of contact for certain customers at certain times.
- Offering special price or product deals exclusively to certain customers.
- Personalizing future mailshots sent. This can be done in various ways: for example, adding an extra enclosure or having a specially worded version of, say, the letter that is part of a shot.

It pays to regard direct mail not as a series of one-off hits, but a developing sequence that grows in strength.

Summary

The key thing here when using direct mail is to keep in mind the broad context, and especially to consider what can be done in ways beyond it, linked to it, yet going further. A good list and carefully planned and executed mailshots may bring in a steady flow of business. But regarding that as a base level and exploring further initiatives can take the whole thing further. If direct mail is a primary technique then this certainly makes sense; if it is part of a complex promotional mix then consideration must be given to how everything works together. This kind of thinking is inherent to all marketing activity where creativity is always important, but so too is a systematic and co-ordinated approach to things on a broadly based foundation.

SUNDAY

MONDAY

TUESDAY

WEDNESDAY

THURSDAY

FRIDAY

SATURDAY

Fact check (answers at the back)

1. When responses come in, how must they be handled?
a) Within a week ❏
b) In a time that will impress ❏
c) Within five days ❏
d) This year ❏

2. Internally, who should see and be familiar with direct mailshots?
a) Only the marketing department ❏
b) Only you ❏
c) Everyone who has customer contact ❏
d) Everyone in the organization ❏

3. What should enquiries (primarily) link to?
a) A celebration ❏
b) Filing ❏
c) The waste-paper basket ❏
d) A clear record system that prompts ongoing action ❏

4. How should you view your mailing list?
a) As one list ❏
b) As a series of categories to be communicated with separately ❏
c) Just another computer file ❏
d) As a mess to be sorted out 'one day' ❏

5. How should information sent to respondents relate to the original shot?
a) No link is necessary ❏
b) It should be identical ❏
c) It should be carefully linked to provide a cohesive overall message ❏
d) It should only be printed in the same colour ❏

6. When you mail the same people regularly, in what way should the shots relate to one another?
a) They can be completely isolated ❏
b) They should appear to be from different organizations ❏
c) They should ignore any continuity ❏
d) They should link neatly to provide continuity ❏

FRIDAY

Email approaches: as easy as 'click'

Some would not regard emails as direct mail, but in modern times they go very much in parallel with it and, while much of what has been said so far applies to them, they deserve a chapter of their own. So, if increased postal costs still rankle, then read on. Emails are a valid way of announcing news, reminding people of your product or services, or selling in a way that prompts a direct response in one of a range of ways, from linking to a website to making a telephone call. Here we review how email marketing can be made effective.

Let's start with one sobering fact: for all that it is useful and ubiquitous, an email can be deleted in a split second, certainly in less time than it takes to tear up a mailshot. In the few seconds when someone looks at your message and decides whether to read on, and takes a moment to do so, what you put in front of them needs to work hard to make that happen. So whether you want to use email as an announcement, a reminder, or to start a dialogue – or as an out-and-out sales message – you must work to make it effective.

When you do so, it can be a powerful method of communication. In addition to seeing emails making announcements, I see them adding a variety of elements to make their regular news interesting. Such messages can start with news. For example, I might send a new review or news of a book moving from hardback to paperback or becoming available in e-form perhaps, but I could add: competitions (I saw one author offering a prize for putting (good!) reviews on Amazon); reviews of books they have read; descriptions of things they have done (a talk or signing session perhaps); advance notice of future events ('Hear me speak at X'). The possibilities are many. Indeed, one of the tasks for anyone doing this sort of thing is to make and keep what is done fresh and interesting every time. Bear in mind here that, while a good deal of information can be sent, the most important part is what shows initially on the recipient's screen. That space is limited and must be well used if people are to be made willing to scroll down.

Of course this is a creative process and thus the possibilities are many, but certain factors tend to help, whatever your style and aims. Consider the following ten 'rules':

1. Be clear what you are trying to achieve

Like any such initiative, email effectiveness benefits from having clear objectives rather than mere pious hopes. Objectives are described specifically in terms of results: they state what you hope will happen and when. It is not a clear objective to try and tell people 'all about a new product', nor does it make it easy to decide on exactly what to say. Saying that you aim to 'prompt at least 20 per cent of recipients to send in orders in the next two to three weeks' is clear and measurable; it can guide you in structuring the message and furthermore you can tell if it happens, and that can assist in refining future 'shots'.

2. Compose a good subject line

This is necessarily brief but needs some thought. Do not put 'Newsletter', 'News' or the product name as a subject; rather, make what you say clear and interesting. Asking a question is a useful approach. For example, I have a new book out titled *How to Make Money from Writing* (Aber Publishing), and in announcing this I might say: 'A new book that can help increase your income' or 'You *can* increase your income' (or more briefly, 'Increase your income'). Or I might phrase it as a question: 'Do you want to increase your writing income?'. The difference here is, I believe, clear.

3. Refine the message content

A good deal has been said already about drafting the text and I will not labour the point about making things clear and attractive again here. Well, other than to say this: make sure you check what you write to avoid errors and ambiguities. And make what you do write succinct. You are not writing an academic essay: your copy needs to be punchy and the overall message must appear – and be – easy to read and manageable. Make it persuasive: it is not enough for you simply to say 'I think it's great'; you need to show evidence.

4. Make it interesting/useful

The key thing here is to think of the recipients and not of yourself. Avoid introspection. Don't start everything with the word 'I' and don't say 'I hope' or even 'I believe'. Have the courage of your convictions: say 'This is ...' or 'This will be ...', and avoid the words 'perhaps,' 'possibly' and 'maybe'. Embellishments such as illustrations must be pertinent and not just thrown in because they are available. It must be clear what they are too; a book cover may be self-explanatory, but other pictures may usefully have captions.

5. Create consistency

Your messages should be consistent. Don't offer a 10 per cent discount off your new book on your website and a different figure in an email, or free postage in one place and not in another. If you have an image, a colour or typeface you use, and that your readers are used to, then continue using it here.

6. Work the list

You can start with existing contacts: everybody from past enquirers to those who have bought from you in the past. Thereafter you can add contacts as names present themselves (some people swap lists), but be careful of listing people who will only see you as a nuisance (see rule 10 below). Updating is important too. People seem to change email addresses quite often, so you need to prune out the 'dead' ones that never reach anyone – what marketers call the hard bounces – and take steps to add corrected addresses or new contacts as replacements to maintain numbers. Remember that some people are important as customers or potential customers, while others are because they can recommend you or assist your publicity.

7. Segment your target

It is said there are two types of people: those who divide people into categories – and the rest. More seriously, because email is so easy to send, time spent doing some sorting into categories may be worthwhile and allow different messages to be sent to different segments of your list. After all, you don't have to juggle envelopes, print different flyers or physically sort papers, so it may be worth sending different messages to past customers/new contacts, men/women, local people/those further afield/those overseas and more, and you can make the separate emails more specific as a result. One category may be only marginally different from another, but it is still worthwhile segmenting in this way to ensure you are addressing people as precisely as possible.

8. Make the call to action clear

If your communication is in any sense promotional then what you ask people *to do* must be absolutely clear. Don't just say, 'Order my product'. Make it clear exactly what they need to do: check details online, send a cheque (specify to what address and made out to whom) and describe any special feature (like giftwrapping, free postage or whatever), listing other details that are important. If there is any confusion here, and if anyone is left feeling they are not quite sure how to proceed, it will quickly be translated into inaction. Make no mistake: once someone puts off taking action, the chances of them restarting it later decline sharply.

9. Test

Everything can be tested: that is, sending one thing to one group and something different to another to see which works best. By the nature of email distribution it is easy to do this. Try experimenting with such facts as price (does a discount work or not; what about free delivery?), colour, layout, text, illustrations and so on, sending one message in one version, another in a different version, and seeing which works. With email it may even make a difference when you send it (the day of the week, or even the time of day) and certainly you may want to avoid, say, a bank holiday. Sometimes testing makes dramatic improvement possible and I know of one case where solely changing the headline on an email increased the percentage response threefold.

10. Avoid being seen as spam and keep it legal

Simple and occasional emailing is unlikely to see you fall foul of the data protection legislation (though for some this may be a consideration). But we all hate spam, and it is a little easier to avoid these days as technological fixes shuttle it away from the main inbox, so be careful to avoid coming over like that or being automatically diverted.

Essentially, email marketing needs to be approved by its recipients, so an 'Unsubscribe' mechanism is necessary and should be included to prevent you getting complaints; so too is sufficient detail about who you are and where the 'shot' comes from. But don't despair: if you mail appropriate people and they find what you say interesting, then they will very often be happy to stay 'on board', as it were, with one proviso – that you do not email them every five minutes. Stating an intended frequency may help people decide whether you are likely to be a nuisance or not, but beware of getting locked in to the 'monthly newsletter' syndrome. It is best only to mail when you have something interesting or useful to say rather than because it is four weeks since you last did so.

Once you are set up and running you will find it is not too difficult to keep ringing the changes; after all, even if you want to send something once a month, you are not looking for too much. Because you are communicating over the Internet you can use the electronic possibilities too: perhaps you could send (or offer free) additional information in the way a consultant of some sort might offer a report or survey to demonstrate their expertise. If you sell through others, retailers say, then such may be linked to them – you offer a coupon that can be printed out and taken into a store to exchange for a discount or something extra. Finally, note that professional help is available in this area. Many people, including me, do not just make up the way they do this, they use a format into which they can slot their own content. Even the standard formats available on recent versions of Word may be useful.

More sophisticated support is available too, providing not just formats but various testing and list management processes. Many companies offer this and, while tailored assistance costs a bit, though it may be worth it, some (including that mentioned) offer standard solutions that will suit many people and are very economical, as well as helping with such elements as personalizing what you send out.

The detail here is (as ever) important. By way of illustration, take a look at a company I have used and like, Little Green Plane, which offers a service to help create effective email shots and a range of best-practice guides and case studies. Go to www.littlegreenplane.com

Summary

All in all, emails are just a specialist form of direct mail and are a way of communicating that many can usefully embrace and use. Email can be quick and easy to implement and avoids, or reduces, more complicated and certainly more expensive communication. It should not be overused, however, or deletion rates will surely rise, but it is well worth a try and, provided it is well done, can put you just a click away from additional sales, revenue and profit.

Fact check (answers at the back)

1. How long does it take for someone to decide to read on or delete an email shot?
   a) One minute ❏
   b) Ten minutes ❏
   c) Two-and-a-half seconds ❏
   d) Ten seconds ❏

2. What factor most quickly turns people off your regular email shots?
   a) Use of bright colours ❏
   b) Over-frequency ❏
   c) Starting with a picture ❏
   d) Poor grammar ❏

3. What is the best subject statement?
   a) One word, e.g. 'News' ❏
   b) Two words, e.g. 'Please read' ❏
   c) A long sentence ❏
   d) Something informative and intriguing ❏

4. What must writing in an email shot be?
   a) Brief ❏
   b) Succinct ❏
   c) Lengthy ❏
   d) Only bullet points ❏

5. Which of the procedural matters here is essential?
   a) The ability to unsubscribe ❏
   b) A questionnaire ❏
   c) A password ❏
   d) Registering *full* details before reading ❏

6. What must your shot not look like?
   a) Ham ❏
   b) Corned beef ❏
   c) Chicken ❏
   d) Spam ❏

7. What must the primary characteristic of any attachment be?
   a) Very long ❏
   b) Clearly interesting and useful ❏
   c) A surprise ❏
   d) Only in black type ❏

8. How should regular email shots make people feel?
   a) Think 'Where's Unsubscribe?' ❏
   b) That the subject line tells them it's irrelevant ❏
   c) That they are always worth a look ❏
   d) They want to delete it ❏

SATURDAY

Future campaigns

If you aim to use direct mail on a continuing basis, then a cycle develops. A campaign is implemented, responses come in and must be dealt with and you find yourself spending time too on originating what comes next: writing copy, designing and printing brochures and all the rest. As you look ahead, here we review two important issues:

- A danger, and a common fault, is allowing ongoing activity to become routine and, at worst, to proceed without sufficient creativity or even thought.
- Future activity must be influenced – accurately influenced – by the experience and results of what has gone before.

Danger ahead

With so much to do, there is a danger that convenience will begin to influence what you do. This can mean working to a formula, ceasing or reducing original thinking and letting the attention to detail that is so important to direct mail slip. All the following might be described as examples of 'ad hoc' marketing, which direct mail users should avoid:

- **Doing something only when there is time.** This is when workload permits you do some new work. But what needs doing must fit not *your* timing, but that inherent in the market and with customers. Failing to maintain continuity can quickly lead to so-called 'feast and famine', a situation with which many organizations are all too familiar where the flow of business becomes erratic. As a result, one minute there can be no prospects to follow and convert, the next – after a burst of activity, a rapidly sent mailshot perhaps – there can be too many simultaneous leads to deal with properly.
- **Convenient action.** This is where activities are favoured because of some particular factor which makes them convenient – *Mary's got some free time this week, let's get her to draft the new letter.* Mary may not be up to it, and the result may either take time to redo or be used yet gather poor results.
- **Subcontracting.** In other words, selecting marketing activity that you can get someone else to do. This seems easy, and is also easy to decide (everyone votes for something that will not involve *them* in any personal hassle). A quarterly newsletter which can be produced externally, perhaps by a public relations consultancy, is a good example. Many organizations have got locked into producing such a thing, then found that mailing it out does not produce good returns, yet stopping it is felt to give negative signs.
- **Familiarity.** Just because you may be good at something does not make it first choice for use. For example, an insurance broker stopped using cartoons on their direct mail material after research showed that their clients viewed them as frivolous and inappropriate, much to the disappointment of the member of staff who loved drawing them and made such things an easy (but not as it proved an appropriate) option.

- **On offer.** Just because something is easily available, for example list rental, does not mean it can be used effectively, much less that it should be used unthinkingly.
- **What is fashionable.** This is a form of copycat action and is never to be recommended (of course you can copy or adapt methodology, but there should always be reason for it beyond simply viewing it as good 'because XYZ does it'). For example, watch the brochures you receive (especially from competitors) and you may see clear signs of copying. It's hardly a sign of original thinking.
- **Perpetuating the same action.** Sometimes a good idea continues in use beyond its sell-by date, as it were, for no other reason than that it has become familiar and thus easy. Given a choice between more of the same and taking time to adapt or innovate, more of the same wins, and wins again, until the method is stale and results confirm this. The antithesis of this can pay dividends.
- **Action unsupported by appropriate skills.** If the personal skills that are involved are inadequate to the task then any good will be, at the least, diluted. For example, although you can write your own copy and do so effectively having studied the principles involved (including here, I hope), this is something you may decide is just not your bag and subcontract (carefully, and remembering that a copywriter can only be as good as the brief they are given).
- **Panic action.** This is never a good idea. If sales drop or competition increases and urgent action is required, then it is even more important than usual that action is thought through. Time spent in reconnaissance is seldom wasted. Ill-considered action, which describes many of the approaches listed here, is never likely to work as well.

The overall rule here is not to allow action to take place on automatic pilot. Every campaign, every mailshot, and every component of every shot, needs to be created on a considered and creative basis. It must be designed to achieve your stated objectives, not dashed off in haste in a way designed only to 'get it done'.

Considered and co-ordinated

Direct mail marketing activity must not be skimped. It must surely be done properly or not done at all. That does not mean that nothing other than elaborate and expensive action will prove useful. The reverse may well be true. But action must be considered. A great deal hangs on it, so it is surely worth some thought both as to how it will be done – the details again – and how it will fit with the rest of your marketing mix.

Ideas are important to all marketing and promotional activity, which continues to be as much an art as a science. The various activities must be well co-ordinated to get the most from them. It is this co-ordination that can help maximize the way every element of even the simplest mix works – where one thing builds on another, adding power and thus constituting a plan of action that is best for one simple reason – it is what works best to bring in the business.

Ongoing fine-tuning

The second thing to consider is, at its simplest, just learning from experience. Given the detail involved, this means analysis of how things are working, carried out in a way that helps make future activity better. The attitude here should be first to test, then to measure on a regular basis and then, if indicated, to fine-tune, adapt or change. The following list should not be regarded as comprehensive, but all these factors are important and illustrate both the overall process and the main elements of the approach. Bear in mind that these factors are all aspects of the shot that can be tested. So what do you check?

- **Headlines.** Wherever they occur (on letters, brochures and so on), headlines are crucial and affect the responses you get disproportionately. I have known mailshots where everything has been kept the same except for a new headline and response rate has jumped massively – for just a few words' difference! So check that these are good (and test).
- **First lines.** Like headlines, these are a key prompt to people reading on and then ultimately responding.
- **Your case.** Is the case you make and the way you describe your product or service clear and suitably descriptive?
- **Benefits.** Are you describing what you offer people in *their* terms – what it will *do* for them or *mean* to them? And does the message remain strong throughout or fade and become bland towards the end?
- **Objections.** Are objections that realistically may come to readers' minds addressed and answered?
- **Figures.** Be sure that any figures used (costs, savings ... whatever) are clearly and accurately expressed; you do not want to say 'about 27%' if that word 'about' makes it sound vague (much less say 'about 27.32%', which sounds ridiculous) and consider also if a descriptive phrase – 'more than 25%' might do a better job.
- **Testimonials.** These must clearly be positive, but they must also match your target audience: are they likely to have heard of their originator and will they find them comparable? A small organization will not necessarily relate to a large one, and vice versa.
- **Guarantee.** You need to make responding sound risk free, so a whole raft of techniques from money back to simply a helpline are important; make sure such arrangements are strongly stated.
- **Avoid negatives.** Describing your service as 'a worry free service' might sound fine, but could still leave the thought of worries in readers' minds. Such statements can be reversed – '100% reliable service' – and may work better, so check.
- **Immediacy.** Be careful of 'allowing time'. An offer 'valid until the end of May' may just allow someone to put things off

(never to go back to it) – urgency and immediacy tend to be better. See how your message sounds in this respect.

- **The PS.** Are you using one? If not, should you? And make sure that any PS is adding emphasis in a useful way.
- **Co-ordination.** Check the overall look. As well as the brochure passing judgement, and the letter and so on, make sure that the overall message spread across the shot hangs together well. There will be some repetition, but there should not be too much and what there is may need wording in different ways.
- **Presentation.** Does it all *look* good? And is it legible? Many a shot has been adversely affected by something as simple as choosing a too-small typeface or colours that confuse and clash.
- **Personal.** Does it sound as if it is addressed to *a recipient*, rather than being an entirely standardized 'all things to all people' approach? Of course, it is clearly going to many people but it should have an individual feel.

It is all too easy to let things run on unchanged – and indeed unconsidered. Reviewing is a habit, a positive one, and one well worth adopting.

If you apply this sort of thinking and analysis item by item (the letter, the brochure, the reply mechanism and so on), and to the overall shot, you can work to ensure that it is all put together as well as possible. Such a process may confirm good work already done, flag up uncertainties (and perhaps the need to test), or lead you to rethink, redraft or redesign the next shot.

Summary

Given the importance of getting the details right (something we have emphasized here regularly), it is worth ending this final day's section with an overall summary of a dozen core points that span the whole content of the book. The following are all crucial to an effective direct mailshot:

1 Systematic selection of names (lists) and careful maintenance of lists.
2 Setting clear objectives for what you want to achieve and ensuring that this influences how you proceed.
3 Matching messages to people.
4 Giving attention to all the individual components: envelope, letter, brochure, etc.
5 Structuring the message so that it is logical and easy to follow.
6 Putting the message in persuasive language.
7 Presenting (layout, etc.) the material as carefully as you write the message.
8 Monitoring regularly and fine-tuning to increase effectiveness in light of experience.
9 Checking to ensure that what is done is strictly cost-effective.

10 Ensuring that what is done
is creatively executed.
11 Keeping those creative approaches
fresh so that what is done does not get
repetitive, dull and stuck in a rut.
12 Keeping it legal (i.e. keeping an eye
on the data protection legislation)
as appropriate.

Finally, if this is not something you
have used previously or extensively,
then remember it is one of the easiest
methodologies to try and test. A small
number of communications to either
past clients or new prospects can get you
embracing an approach that may well
become a significant part of your overall
promotional mix.

Fact check (answers at the back)

1. How much preparation time should you allow?
   - a) Sufficient to get every detail right ❏
   - b) A week ❏
   - c) Ten hours ❏
   - d) Whatever you can spare ❏

2. How must creating the material be done?
   - a) In haste ❏
   - b) On automatic pilot ❏
   - c) With due consideration ❏
   - d) In the moments between everything else ❏

3. Which characteristic must what you send always retain?
   - a) Freshness ❏
   - b) The same thing every time ❏
   - c) Inoffensiveness ❏
   - d) Blandness ❏

4. Why can repeated use of tried and tested ways be wrong?
   - a) It saves time ❏
   - b) It needs no thought ❏
   - c) It gets stale ❏
   - d) It's easier and cheaper ❏

5. Why is fine-tuning your approach essential?
   - a) It wastes time ❏
   - b) It risks inappropriate repetition ❏
   - c) It keeps you on target ❏
   - d) It's not necessary ❏

6. How should you view a final check?
   - a) As useful ❏
   - b) As a chore ❏
   - c) To be done if time permits ❏
   - d) As essential ❏

7. Making a shot effective demands what?
   - a) Luck ❏
   - b) Appropriate skill ❏
   - c) Guesswork ❏
   - d) A haphazard approach ❏

8. Which of the following elements should your message *not* contain?
   - a) Benefits ❏
   - b) Evidence ❏
   - c) Testimonials ❏
   - d) Negatives ❏

7 × 7

1 Seven key ideas

- Direct marketing is a particular type of promotion and success is in the details.
- Key to success is the quality of your lists: the people to whom you direct your promotion.
- It is easy to measure the results of direct marketing, so fine-tune your approaches through testing and experiment.
- To be consistently effective, always make every element of the 'shot' work together.
- To make your messages truly persuasive, allow yourself enough time to create and develop them.
- Use the 'tricks of the trade' (using the research about what devices work) but on a considered basis, directed at your specific target audience.
- By all means go electronic, but take care: it is easy to dash off emailed messages and dilute their effectiveness.

2 Seven of the best resources

- Royal Mail offers a variety of advice and hints about techniques as well as offering special postage rates for business. www.royalmail.com/business
- The Direct Marketing Association is the professional body for those working in this sector, and a source of help and advice. www.dma.org.uk
- The Chartered Institute of Marketing is the overall body for marketing professionals; it offers help, advice and professional qualifications. www.cim.co.uk
- The Data Protection Register is the starting point for investigating all the legalities of data protection. www.gove.uk/data-protection-register-ico-personal-data

- The Advertising Standards Authority is a useful point of reference about what is and is not permitted in advertising of all sorts. www.asa.org.uk
- If you feel the need, this website is a source of freelance copywriters. http://procopywritersnetwork.co.uk
- Other peoples' direct mail: keep a file of the best (and worst) of what you receive. It can form a useful reference – the best not to copy slavishly but to spur thinking and prompt ideas, and the worst to remind you of what not to do.

3 Seven things to avoid

- Using inappropriate or otherwise inadequate lists
- Not testing
- Not checking – proofreading – carefully (several times)
- Failing to focus on customers and being too introspective in your messages
- Breaking the rules (there is much research about what works, so use it)
- Following the rules too slavishly (remember that this is a *creative* process)
- Failing to link all aspects of the shot together

4 Seven inspiring people

- Drayton Bird: the ultimate guru on direct marketing, whose books *Commonsense Direct & Digital Marketing* and *How to Write Sales Letters that Sell* (Kogan Page) are a must
- David Ogilvy: the grandfather of advertising whose book *Ogilvy on Advertising* (Prion Books) is useful for anyone involved in this area
- The people who originated the direct mail from *Reader's Digest* over the years: it is not a style that should be slavishly copied, but everyone can learn something from it

- Stephen Heffer: associate editor of *The Daily Telegraph*, who has helped improve writing standards with his book *Strictly English* (Random House); anyone writing copy should take an interest in language

- Keith Waterhouse: the late novelist and columnist, who was passionate about language and whose book about grammar, *English our English* (Penguin), is as funny as it is useful. It is out of print but worth tracking down online.

- Philip Kotler: instrumental in the development of marketing and probably the ultimate overall marketing guru. Even if you are focusing on a subsection of marketing, he is worth reading – try *Kotler on Marketing* (Free Press).

- John Gribbin: this science writer may seem an odd person to include here, but he is renowned for the clarity of his writing. Clarity is everything in direct marketing because no one will buy anything they do not understand, so observing how a master makes complexity clear is useful to the copywriter. Try his *In Search of the Multiverse* (Allen Lane).

5 Seven great quotes

- 'God is on the side not of the heavy battalions, but of the best shot.' Voltaire

- 'Sell the benefits, not your company or product. People buy results, not features.' Jay Abraham

- 'Give 'em what they never knew they wanted.' Diana Vreeland

- 'I don't sell cosmetics, I sell hope.' Elizabeth Arden

- 'Advertising isn't a science. It's persuasion. And persuasion is an art.' Bill Bernbach

- 'What is written without effort is in general read without pleasure.' Samuel Johnson

- Usp Needham's creative advertising guidelines:
  'Break the pattern.'
  'Position the product clearly and competitively.'
  'Reflect the character of the product.'

'Appeal to both head and heart.'
'Generate trust.'
'Speak with one voice.'

6 Seven things to do today

- Find time to review recent activity.
- Read over your last mail (or electronic) shot and critique it honestly.
- List changes you might make.
- Schedule adequate time to prepare your next shot and mark it out in your diary.
- Think about lists – to whom exactly your next shot will go.
- Think about testing: are there things with which you could experiment (e.g. a long or short letter)?
- Sleep on it; anything like this is best revisited before it is finalized.

7 Seven trends for tomorrow

- Even if economies improve, markets will remain volatile and competitive.
- The 'electronic' aspect of promotion will become more varied and complex.
- Customer loyalty will remain uncertain and need winning and holding.
- Postage costs will increase ahead of other things.
- Pressure on time will remain, or increase, yet the details must still be right and this does not just happen.
- Channels of distribution, with which direct marketing must interact, will continue to change.
- Changes likely to affect this style of business will continue to occur and the rate of change will increase.

Further reading

At the core of this subject is effective writing, so a first recommendation here is to have a dictionary and thesaurus to hand. Next, you may find a totally biased recommendation useful: three books I have written fit here:

- *Successful Pitching for Business In A Week* (John Murray Learning, 2013)
- *How to Write Reports and Proposals* (Kogan Page, 2013)
- *Persuasive Writing for Business* (Bookshaker, 2014)

I also recommend:

- *Common Sense Direct and Digital Marketing*, Drayton Bird (Kogan Page, 2007)

This is the work of the real guru of direct mail, now in its fifth edition and incorporating the digital aspect too; it is excellent.